FROM PROPS TO JETS

Commercial Aviation's Transition to the Jet Age 1952-1962

JON PROCTOR, MIKE MACHAT and *CRAIG KODERA*

specialtypress
PUBLISHERS AND WHOLESALERS

SpecialtyPRESS
PUBLISHERS AND WHOLESALERS

Specialty Press
39966 Grand Avenue
North Branch, MN 55056
Phone: 651-277-1400 or 800-895-4585
Fax: 651-277-1203
www.specialtypress.com

Edit by Mike Machat
Layout by Monica Seiberlich

ISBN 978-1-58007-146-8
Item No. SP146

Library of Congress Cataloging-in-Publication Data

Proctor, Jon.
    From props to jets : commercial aviation's transition to the jet age 1952-1962 / by by Jon Proctor, Mike Machat, and Craig Kodera.
        p. cm.
    Includes index.
    ISBN 978-1-58007-146-8
    1. Transport planes—History—20th century. 2. Aeronautics, Commercial—History—20th century. 3. Airlines—History—20th century. I. Machat, Mike. II. Kodera, Craig. III. Title.
    TL685.4.P76 2010
    387.7'334909045—dc22
                                        2009048767

Printed in China
10 9 8 7 6 5 4 3 2 1

Distributed in the UK and Europe by
Crécy Publishing Ltd
1a Ringway Trading Estate
Shadowmoss Road
Manchester M22 5LH England
Tel: 44 161 499 0024
Fax : 44 161 499 0298
www.crecy.co.uk
enquiries@crecy.co.uk

On the Front Cover:
A new era begins as the first Douglas DC-8 jetliner takes to the skies on May 30, 1958. Lifting off at Long Beach, this aircraft ushered in the Jet Age for the world's premier builder of commercial airliners. Sadly, that title would not last another decade. (Jon Proctor Collection)

On the Front Cover (lower left):
Luxurious cabin service in the 1950s is depicted here as a stewardess serves passengers aboard a Trans Canada Airlines Lockheed Constellation. (Courtesy of Scott Bloom)

On the Front Cover (lower right):
Routes covered today by what are known as "regional jets" were flown in the 1950s by twin-engine propliners like this Braniff Convair 340. (Bob Woodling)

On the Back Cover (top):
The airplane that shrank the world, Boeing's 707 Intercontinental, carried 150 passengers over distances of 4,000 miles at speeds of 600 mph. It was the first jet airliner to link all the world's continents. (Mike Machat)

On the Back Cover (bottom):
The zenith of piston-powered airliners, this Douglas DC-7 could fly nonstop across the United States in only eight hours—a far cry from the early days of air travel when Ford Trimotors flew during the daytime only, and trains made the night legs. (Mike Machat Collection)

On the Title Page:
"First Jet." Painted by co-author Craig Kodera before he became a pilot for American Airlines, this depiction of that company's first Boeing 707 (N7501A) captures the drama and excitement of the first U.S. transcontinental jet service in 1959. (Copyright Craig Kodera)

On Facing Page:
Complete with streamlined wingtip tanks, TWA's Lockheed Super-G Constellation epitomized elegant commercial air travel in the mid 1950s. Well-dressed passengers are shown deplaning at the airline's base in Kansas City. (Wings & Airpower/Mike Machat Collection)

CONTENTS

ACKNOWLEDGMENTS

I grew up in an airline family. My father was a pioneering airmail pilot, taking advantage of his World War I flight training to secure a job with the then-new Colonial Western Airways, which eventually melded with what we know today as American Airlines. As a young lad riding on passes with my family, I remember the look on ticket agents' faces as they noted Dad's payroll number: 02.

I absolutely owe my love of the industry to him, along with my desire to write; Dad had a great way with words and wrote stories for several publications. I recently discovered the first two chapters of a book he was planning to author but never finished. What I wouldn't give for a chance to sit down with him today and fill in the missing holes.

To a greater degree, my brother Bill, a retired TWA pilot, and his wife Ann, get most of the credit for encouraging me to pursue my own airline career. Bill loaned me aviation books, paid the extra "jet surcharge" so I could take my first ride in a Boeing 707, and has provided so much support and answers to my endless questions. Many thanks go to him, my best friend.

Although Robert Serling refers to me as his mentor and role model, it really has been the other way around. Bob is a true inspiration to all aviation writers, and always finds time to take my calls and provide sage advice. He readily shares a wealth of knowledge and can be counted on for straightforward responses when acting as a sounding board for my book and story ideas. But above all, he is a treasured friend.

In addition to Bob, I was fortunate enough to meet three of my biggest aviation heroes who are no longer with us: Jimmy Doolittle, C. R. Smith, and Paul Tibbets. Close friendships formed with people in the airline industry are too many to list here, but each has been an inspiration, adding to a wonderful career in aviation.

Finally, special thanks are offered to the co-authors I am so lucky to have as great personal friends.

— Jon Proctor

As with any labor of love, there are many people who helped along the way, and without whom, a project such as this simply would not have been possible. Starting with the "big picture," my thanks to Donald Wills Douglas for all his great airliners, and to my father for cherished memories of a flight aboard an Eastern DC-7B Golden Falcon, which planted the seed. Coming West from New York to California to work as a young artist for the proud company Mr. Douglas founded was nothing less than the fulfillment of a life-long dream.

I also would not have had the career I enjoy today without the inspiration of my uncle, George Hildebrand. His 32-year career as a chief engineer and program manager with Republic Aviation Corporation served as the ultimate source for my insatiable desire to become part of America's burgeoning aerospace industry. As a proud designer of military jet fighters, he held airliners in a different regard, but gained new and heartfelt respect for commercial aviation when my budding career at Douglas began to emulate his own.

The man to whom I owe a large debt of gratitude for connecting me with the literary world is R.E.G. Davies, former Curator of Air Transport for the Smithsonian National Air and Space Museum, and one-time member of the marketing analysis team at McDonnell Douglas in Long Beach. Ron and I have worked together on 15 airline history books, and he has written many of the definitive reference works on the history of the world's airline industry. Ironically, many of Davies' books served as invaluable and ironclad reference sources for this project.

My admiration, respect, and thanks to John Wegg, world's foremost authority on the magnificent Sud Caravelle, for years of collaboration on many inspirational projects together, and for setting the gold standard in modern airline writing. The late Terry Waddington showed me how pure passion for a product and deep love for the airline industry translated into impressive sales of McDonnell Douglas jetliners. Special thanks to Tony Landis, Dennis Jenkins, and Joshua Stoff. Finally, to my two cohorts, Jon Proctor and Craig Kodera, go heartfelt appreciation for a collaborative effort on this project that has exceeded expectations. I am most grateful to have aviation friends of this caliber.

— Mike Machat

Over the years I have had the uncommon privilege of being associated with the world of aviation and, in particular, that of commercial aviation. My uncle Harry Botterud was maintenance supervisor for Los Angeles Airways in the 1950s; my father spent a lifelong career in the aerospace industry, the last half of which was at Douglas Aircraft in the Commercial Division at Long Beach. I managed to work at Douglas myself after college and prior to joining the Air Force Reserve, thanks to Dad.

Our neighborhood was filled with airline pilots, one of whom was Gary Ferguson of Continental, who bought me my first instructional ride in a Cessna 150 at Meadowlark Airport in Huntington Beach. This led to my licensure to fly airplanes at age 17. My mentor and guide into the life of aviation, Bob Brandt of L. A. Airways (1960s version), introduced me to his old flying buddy, Scott Bergey, who was late of Air California.

Thanks to these two men, I managed to find myself flying at Air Cal, later to be merged with American Airlines, thus fulfilling my long-hoped-for childhood dream. Nine thousand hours of flying time later, here we are.

Meadowlark has since been turned into homes. Douglas is now Boeing, and both Dad and Gary Ferguson have flown west. I no longer inhabit the cockpit of an airplane, but to have witnessed what I have in my lifetime… the grandeur of proud people crafting entire industries for the betterment of all on this planet, and the momentous positive change among its peoples, I am fortunate. To be able to now write about what I have known all my life makes me humble. So my thanks extend to you, our special readers.

And most significantly, thanks of a very special kind to my dearest of friends, the co-authors of this book.

— Craig Kodera

DEDICATION

This book is respectfully dedicated to the memory of Terry Waddington, aeronautical engineer, Douglas Aircraft Company salesman par excellence, and one of the last of the true believers.

FOREWORD

No one is better qualified to write the dramatic story of air travel's transition from propellers to jet-power than Jon Proctor, Mike Machat, and Craig Kodera. They constitute a trio of respected chroniclers of aviation history. Forgive me, however, if I emphasize that Jon Proctor has been my mentor and role model for many years, someone to whom I have turned to many times for help with my own historical research. What is more important is that this talented trio has fashioned a work that is factually honest, scrupulously objective, and blessed with a rare "we-were-there" insight.

From Props To Jets takes us back to what arguably was the most dramatic and significant decade in civil aviation history: the saga of the 1952 to 1962 technological revolution that literally shrank the world by measuring distance in terms of hours rather than days and miles traveled. This brilliantly researched and written contribution to aviation history could not come at a more appropriate time, for it injects into the doom-and-gloom atmosphere of today's air travel difficulties and complaints, a reminder of accomplishments that we now take for granted. It also accents the positives instead of the negatives, something that is rare and sorely needed in this era of adversarial journalism. For as the authors point out, this was also the decade during which the airplane itself supplanted the family automobile, bus, train, and ship as the single most dominant provider of long-distance travel.

I owe these fine writers my gratitude for producing not merely a fascinating book but an important one. The airline world that people like Jon, Mike, Craig, and I respected and loved, even when we criticized it, exists no more. This book, therefore, comes poignantly close to being a kind of requiem, a magnificent and justified tribute to an industry that has always taken ten steps forward for every step backward, and ultimately deserved a far better fate.

— **Robert J. Serling**
Former Aviation Editor,
United Press International

ABOUT THE AUTHORS

Jon Proctor, a seasoned veteran of the airline industry, served in various positions with Trans World Airlines (TWA) for 27 years and comes from an aviation family; his father was a pioneering pilot for American Airlines and his brother flew for TWA. He has written two books and numerous magazine articles on commercial aviation over the years and is also the former editor of *AIRLINERS* magazine. Jon contributed many of his stunning original airline photographs for use in this book.

Mike Machat is a former aviation artist and staff illustrator for the Douglas Aircraft Company, and served as editor of *Wings & Airpower* magazine. Known for his love of commercial aviation, Mike has also designed airline color schemes for DC-9 and DC-10 aircraft, painted airliner-model boxtops, and illustrated numerous books on airliners and airline history. Having flown in every type of airliner from the Ford Trimotor to the Concorde, Mike brings a wealth of commercial aviation experience to this project.

Craig Kodera has lived a life immersed in aviation as the son of an engineer for Douglas Aircraft. Craig realized his dream of becoming an airline pilot having flown for both Air California and American Airlines, and also served as a transport and tanker pilot in the U.S. Air Force. Additionally, he is a world-class aviation artist whose artwork has been published by The Greenwich Workshop and who counts among his commercial aviation clients McDonnell Douglas and Airbus Industrie.

INTRODUCTION

The 1950s was an incredible decade to be living in America. With World War II fading into distant memory, the country entered a prosperous and momentous era with a clear emphasis on the future. Military supersonic flight was now a matter of routine and visions of manned space travel entered the public consciousness for the very first time, but the most revolutionary aspect of all this futurism was the turbine engine. Just mentioning the word "jet" conjured up visions of great speed and power or snow-white contrails seen against a stratospheric blue sky, and the mass public seemed suddenly swept up in the great expectations of the new futuristic Jet Age.

Before World War II, the mere thought of an airline passenger purchasing a ticket and boarding a jet-powered airliner to fly to some exotic far-off locale at nearly 600 mph would have been pure science fiction. Then, in May 1952, Britain's elegant de Havilland Comet 1 boarded its first passengers and took to the European skies. Although the commercial Jet Age didn't begin in earnest until 1959, the die had been cast and airline passengers were soon flying at speeds and altitudes once strictly the domain of record-breaking military test pilots, little more than a decade earlier. A major difference, however, is that these lucky passengers were dining on four-star cuisine surrounded by sublime luxury while flying at speeds approaching Mach 1!

This book celebrates the magical years from 1952 to 1962 with an in-depth look at the amazing machines that made commercial jet flight possible, as seen from the perspective of the propeller-driven aircraft that were in worldwide service prior to the introduction of the jets. The span of time from the zenith of piston-powered luxury airliners to the world's first intercontinental jetliners was only five short years, but this paradigm shift in powerplants, speed, and luxury revolutionized air travel forever.

So fasten your seatbelt, sit back, relax, and enjoy the ride as authors Jon Proctor, Mike Machat, and Craig Kodera take you along for literary flights in the world's most luxurious propliners and pioneering first-generation jetliners, using magnificent original color photography from their respective collections coupled with industry-wide photos and memorabilia. It will be a memorable journey steeped in airline nostalgia and history, and will probably make you long once again for this incredible era in aviation that is, sadly, now gone forever.

Distilled water, injected into the Pratt & Whitney JT3C turbojets to augment thrust, produces heavy black smoke as a brand-new American Airlines 707 Jet Flagship lifts off the runway for another transcontinental flight in 1959. (Charlie Atterbury)

Chapter One

SETTING THE STAGE
(1946-1950)

Flagship Knoxville, *an American Airlines Douglas DC-3 in 1939.* (Craig Kodera/The Greenwich Workshop)

After World War II ended, the world entered an era of recovery and rebuilding. Commercial air transportation began to expand using fleets of surplus military transports and leftover prewar passenger aircraft. Despite there being a number of false hopes with giant new airliner concepts that never came to fruition, the promise of bigger and better airliners was looming on the distant horizon. Maybe someday, there would even be jets.

Evolution of Post–World War II Airliners— USAAF Surplus

The end of World War II saw a massive transfer of aircraft to the airline industry, mostly Douglas C-47s reconfigured to passenger layouts. In addition to civil DC-3s returning from military service, more than 9,000 C-47s were available to choose from, at prices less than $10,000 each.

In addition, 1,100 Douglas DC-4s, built as C-54s for the Army and R5Ds for the Navy, became available and were purchased by airlines in large numbers. American Airlines acquired 50 C-54s at the standard government price of $90,000 each, and spent an additional $175,000 per airplane to install passenger interiors. Pan Am, which had ordered DC-4s in 1940, went on to fly 90 of the type, while other carriers purchased smaller numbers.

Powered by four Pratt & Whitney R-2000 engines, the DC-4 rumbled along at a maximum speed of 227 mph and possessed near-transatlantic range, but was chiefly used on shorter domestic routes, carrying 44 passengers in a standard configuration, plus two pilots and one or two flight attendants. In addition to American, surplus DC-4s were acquired early on by Delta, Eastern, Northwest, Pan Am, TWA, and United.

As the war ended, Douglas built a small batch of civil DC-4s before concentrating on production of its new DC-6, which airlines would begin receiving in

A crowd gathers around this TWA-painted Constellation after its record-breaking, 6-hour 58-minute flight from Burbank to National Airport in Washington, D.C., on April 17, 1944, with Howard Hughes and Jack Frye at the controls. Although it was scheduled for handover to the War Department, Hughes was allowed the airplane for the cross-country flight and, without permission, had his airline's colors applied to complete the publicity coup. The loading steps, made of wood, were specially constructed and painted for the event. This would be the only Constellation to wear Transcontinental Line markings, and it never flew in revenue service with TWA. (TWA/Jon Proctor Collection)

In 1948, LaGuardia Airport in Queens, New York, drew thousands of weekend onlookers with its panoramic observation deck. (Peter Black Collection)

April 16, 1944, Las Vegas, Nevada. TWA Treasurer John Lockhart, acting on behalf of the U.S. Army Air Force, accepts the flight manual and paperwork as the first Lockheed Constellation is turned over to the airline. A variation of the Constellation logo, with added stars, is visible on the Connie, along with a tailskid that was only fitted on the first few airplanes. Wearing military registration 310310, the airplane was immediately flown back to Burbank and prepared for its record-breaking flight to Washington, D.C., the following day. Note boarding ladder. (Craig Kodera Collection)

1947. Western Air Lines was a factory-delivery DC-4 customer. At Burbank, California, Lockheed began producing civil variants of its Constellation after diverting the type to the military during the war. C-69 Constellations were handed over to TWA and Pan Am, both hungry to replenish their small fleets and add capacity as postwar prosperity began rapid growth in air travel.

On U.S. domestic routes, TWA gained a significant advantage over its domestic rivals, as even the ex-military Connies were on a par with the DC-6s yet to arrive. Fifteen of these larger, more-modern airliners required less modification work than the C-54s and had the advantage of pressurized cabins that allowed them to cruise at higher altitudes to avoid bad weather. Eighteen-cylinder, Wright Cyclone R-3350 radial engines permitted cruising altitudes of 21,000 feet. Accommodations for up to 57 passengers were provided on daylight flights, with sleeping berths added for longer night and transatlantic flights.

The type was used to inaugurate TWA's transatlantic service in February 1946 and quickly spread to domestic routes as well, supplementing five four-engine Boeing 307 Stratoliners that were returned to TWA from military duty in 1944. The C-69s were followed by civil-built Model 049 Connies. TWA also acquired 15 C-54s for transatlantic use through purchase and lease contracts.

A Pan American World Airways Stratocruiser, its landing gear already retracting into the wells, departs from Los Angeles on June 23, 1950, bound for Honolulu. At the west end of Runways 25-Left and -Right, traffic on bordering Sepulveda Boulevard was stopped for long-range takeoffs in the days before a tunnel was built under the runways to allow extension of the strips. The Stratocruiser remains to this day the most successful adaptation of a military transport (the C-97) into a luxury airliner. (Los Angeles World Airports)

State of the Industry: Rebuilding Fleets, Markets and the Boeing 377

Although surplus military transports served to boost postwar capacity, airline managers envisioned even greater growth and ordered newer, modern aircraft to meet demand and improve performance. While new DC-6s began entering the market, Lockheed upgraded its Constellation, boosting weight and range in the form of the 749 and 749A variants. These types found work in transatlantic service and to Hawaii from the West Coast.

Meanwhile, the Boeing Company utilized its military B-29 design to bring about a civil version, the Model 377 Stratocruiser, combining the bomber's wings and an enlarged fuselage that featured sleeping berths, dressing rooms, and a lower-deck passenger compartment used as a lounge. Power came from four 3,500-hp Pratt & Whitney R-4360 Double Wasp turbocharged engines, by far the largest and most complicated civilian reciprocal powerplants of the time. These engines gave the 377 a service ceiling of 35,000 feet and a range of more than 4,000 miles. At 25,000 feet it could cruise at between 300 and 340 mph.

The "Strat" was first utilized on Hawaiian routes by Northwest, Pan American, and United; Pan Am also introduced the type on transatlantic flights. Within the continental United States, the larger-capacity airliners were pressed into service on medium- and long-haul routes. Curiously, all three types had transcontinental nonstop capability but, as we will learn, coast-to-coast nonstops were still several years away.

The "Might Have Beens"

The sky was the limit for dreaming about giant new airliners, with impressive experimental prototypes designed at the end of World War II. A double-decker six-engine goliath from Convair; a four-engine military transport conversion from Douglas; a sleek 450-mph whippet of an airplane from Republic, and a mammoth eight-engine "Queen of the Skies" from Great Britain all shared one thing in common: They never flew as an airliner!

Republic XR-12 Rainbow

The sleek and exotic Republic XR-12 was an airplane well ahead of its time in 1946. Still the fastest four-engine piston-powered airplane ever flown, the XR-12 was envisioned as a long-range, high-altitude photoreconnaissance aircraft capable of taking high-definition aerial photographs day or night, and developing those images onboard the aircraft while in flight. With a top speed of more than 460 mph, the XR-12 also offered unheard-of performance for the world's leading airlines with a 44-passenger commercial version named the RC-2 Rainbow, an airplane that promised near-jet-like performance and a 4,000-mile range. Unfortunately, that promise went unfulfilled due to the cancellation of the XR-12's military mission coupled with declining postwar airline economics.

Often mistaken for a more modern turboprop, the XR-12 was powered by four Pratt & Whitney R-4360 Twin Wasps—the same engines as Boeing's venerable Stratocruiser. However, with its more streamlined aerodynamics and lighter overall gross weight, the XR-12 enjoyed an almost-100-mph speed advantage. Although two military prototypes actually flew, the airliner version never got off the drawing boards despite being ordered by both American Airlines and Pan American World Airways. The cold realities of postwar economics rendered the Rainbow as being too costly at $1.25 million each, when surplus C-54s were suddenly flooding the market and being sold for $100,000 apiece. It was sadly ironic that Republic's only activity in the airliner game was in winning a contract from American to refurbish and outfit its newly purchased surplus C-54s!

Although neither exists today, the two prototypes built by Republic exceeded all design specifications. The right airplane at the wrong time, the XR-12 became another of aviation's mysterious dead ends, and a graphic example of a successful—and in this case *unparalleled*—aircraft not making it into series production. (Even its name was a clever play on words signaling the end of war's storm clouds brought about with the help of the company's Thunderbolt fighters.) Considered as Republic Chief Engineer Alexander Kartveli's ultimate masterpiece, the Rainbow was one of the most elegant and graceful looking airplanes ever built. But for world economics and timing, it could have been a legend!

Looking like a much more modern airplane than one designed in 1944, the magnificent Republic XR-12 long-range photo-recon prototype was in a class by itself. The RC-2 commercial version would have offered airlines near-jet-like performance with its ability to fly 450 mph at altitudes of up to 40,000 feet. The XR-12 achieved a top speed of 471 mph—the highest speed ever attained by a multi-engine piston-powered aircraft in level flight. (Mike Machat Collection)

American Airlines, along with Pan American, placed provisional orders for the RC-2 Rainbow. This period advertisement gave airline passengers a glimpse into the future. (Craig Kodera Collection)

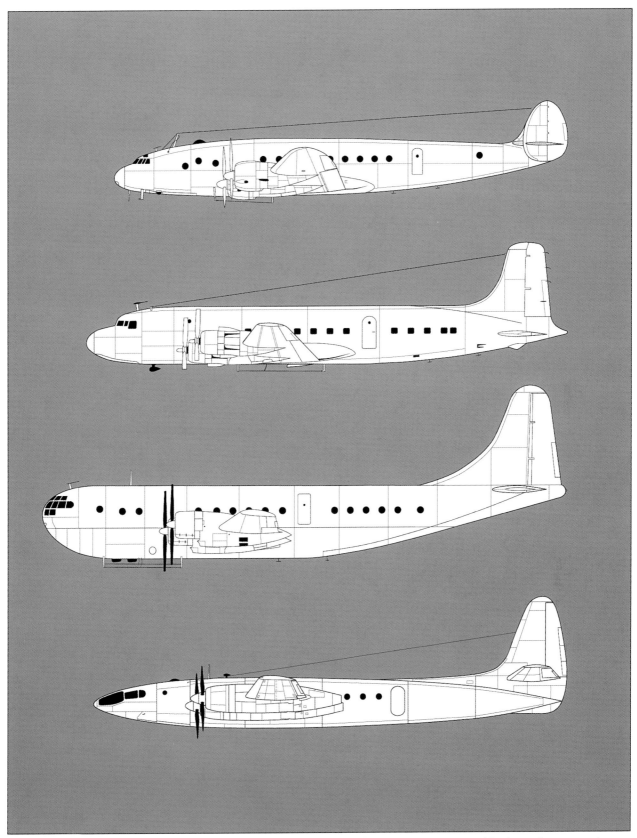

Nicely showing the size and shape comparison of the Rainbow with its contemporaries, this chart gives a good snapshot of the airliners of the time. From top to bottom: Lockheed 749 Constellation, Douglas DC-6, Boeing 377 Stratocruiser, and Republic RC-2 Rainbow. (Digital artwork by Tony R. Landis)

Original Douglas DC-7 (C-74 for the Air Force)

During the war years, Pan American World Airways was preparing for the day when hostilities would end and it could reclaim its vaunted position as leader of the world's international air lines. One of the first of its new "Super Clipper" aircraft ideas sprang from the Douglas C-74 Globemaster cargo aircraft being designed as part of the logistics and supply network for the U. S. Army Air Force.

The Globemaster was a large airplane, which suited Pan Am's style of service quite elegantly. It would carry 108 passengers plus a crew of 13, and could fly nonstop from New York to points in South America, its intended routing. The cabin was to be divided into two sections, one accommodating 36 passengers, and the other 72. An onboard fully powered galley for hot meals was on the list, as were the typically grand dressing rooms and toilets expected on a Pan Am Clipper.

Pan American announced an order for what was to be known as the Douglas DC-7 on October 23, 1944: a commitment for 26 aircraft at a cost of $40 million. This was a staggering amount of money and airplanes in the mid-1940s, but as was typical of the airline and Juan Trippe who ran it, nothing was ever done in a small way at Pan Am.

Unfortunately, although the C-74 was built in one short production run and contributed years of great service with the Air Force, the "DC-7" never made it into the Pan American fleet owing to the fact that the airline reevaluated its service level requirements. Gigantic and spacious luxury just wasn't profitable in the postwar climate, and the airline began its landplane service with the Douglas DC-4 and Lockheed Constellation instead.

Convair Model 37 (XC-99 for the Air Force)

As early as 1942, the Army Air Force was interested in a cargo version of the Convair XB-36 bomber, and let a contract for one aircraft in December of that year. This airplane was to share the wings, engines, tail surfaces, and landing gear of the bomber, but have an entirely new two-deck fuselage to accommodate troops and cargo. The same aircraft configured for commercial passenger carriage was an obvious spin-off and was offered to the airlines during the war.

In February 1945, Pan American World Airways ordered 15 of the commercial transports for construction and delivery following war's end. The airplanes were to be configured to carry 204 passengers and 15,300 pounds of mail, cargo, and luggage. Airspeed at cruise was forecast to come in at just under 300 mph, and range could be assumed to easily cover a 4,000-mile trip. The seating in the upper cabin was five abreast, intermixed with sleeping berths and day airplane seats. Lounges were to be located on each deck, and a spiral

This is the exact scale model of the so-called DC-7 to have been used by Pan American World Airways in its postwar transatlantic operations. With a wingspan greater than the height of a 16-story building, the new airplane would have been seven times the size of a DC-3. The new Clipper was to have carried 108 passengers and a crew of 10 at speeds of more than 300 mph, offering lower seat-mile costs than ever before. (Craig Kodera Collection)

The long and short of it for Convair in the early 1950s is represented in this ramp photo taken at San Diego's Lindbergh Field. The double-decker XC-99 transport literally dwarfs the small L-13 Liaison and Observation plane, but ironically, neither type ever entered production. (National Archives via Dennis R. Jenkins)

staircase stood at the fore and aft ends of the cabin to connect these decks. A large galley was also planned for the airplane, and spa-like lavatories would cater to the needs of passengers.

Interestingly enough, even at this early date in the world's advancement of aviation, the Model 37 was envisioned as being powered by Wright T-35 turboprop engines. Unfortunately, that powerplant did not come to fruition, and the standard Pratt & Whitney R-4360 piston engines were left in place, as with the B-36 installation. In the end, this design element allowed the XC-99 to be forever known as the world's largest piston-powered cargo aircraft. As an airliner, the airplane would have been the first of the 747 style jumbo aircraft winging over the globe. The world would wait another 25 years to experience such an aircraft, however, as Pan American once again realized that bigger wasn't necessarily better in the postwar environment. In the meantime, the airline contented itself with the less ambitious Boeing Stratocruiser as its premier Clipper to span the oceans.

Bristol Type 167 Brabazon

Perhaps most ambitious within the Luxury Airliner category of contestants, Bristol's Brabazon Mark One airliner was a true behemoth in all regards. The aerodynamic answer to the question of more passengers and more range was, in those days of World War II and immediately thereafter, to simply take a given, typical airplane shape along with the ratio of its parts, and inflate them. For instance, if you need more lift to carry

all that new payload, simply design a giant wing to do so. Or a bigger fuselage and tail group to handle more passengers. Hence the Brabazon was a *very* large aircraft in all proportions. So large, in fact, that Bristol had to lengthen the runway at its Filton works, which necessitated the destruction of an entire village in order to build on to the pavement. Also, two new production hangars were constructed to produce these giants. The wing camber was so thick and high that a man could easily walk upright through the center wing area had it been open, and each wing had a bumper on its underside tip to absorb the inevitable runway impact during a crosswind operation.

The Type 167 was named after Lord Brabazon, an influential aeronaut cum aviation booster who chaired the committee that bore his name during World War II. That group of men laid the groundwork for all the future postwar airliners that Britain should produce, with differing specifications for differing roles. The largest airplane would be the transatlantic flag carrier. Thus, as Bristol embarked on the building of the great international airliner in March 1943, it seemed only appropriate to name it for its founding mentor.

The Brabazon had a wingspan of 229 feet, cruised with its low-speed airfoil shape at a stately 250 mph, and could carry up to 180 pampered passengers in compartmentalized style on two separate decks. Bristol and British Overseas Airways Corporation (BOAC) liked to compare the interior of the airplane to that of a luxury salon railway car, offering a lavish 200 square feet of luxury space per passenger (in the 100-passenger

A rare color picture of the massive Bristol Type 167 Brabazon reflects its 229-foot wingspan and dual Centaurus engines buried inside the wings. Aircraft is seen during a test run at Bristol's Filton, England, plant. (BAE Systems)

configuration) so as to help them survive the interminably long flights across the North Atlantic. As with the other aircraft we are discussing in this section, the Brabazon was striving to be the "last word" in air travel in the late 1940s. Features included a cinema, lounge, bar, and ladies' dressing room, not to mention impeccable British service.

Among the advanced features of the Brabazon, all flight controls were 100-percent hydraulically powered, and it was the first airplane to be so designed. The dual Bristol Centaurus engines per each nacelle were actually buried inside the wing, each at an angle to a central driveshaft turning contra-rotating propellers. Production aircraft, starting with the Mark Two air-

frame, were to be even more advanced powered by Proteus turboprop engines.

Putting this airplane into context, it first flew in 1949, just after the de Havilland Comet made its maiden flight. The contrast could not be more stunning, and served a harbinger of things to come for the "Brab" as BOAC lost all interest in the airplane. British European Airways (BEA) wanted to fly the one-and-only airframe (the never-fully-completed number two aircraft was scrapped) on its service to Paris, but fatigue problems associated with the propeller mountings and an overall flight time limitation of 5,000 hours scotched the idea of revenue passenger flying. By October 1953, the Mark One airframe was broken up for scrap as well.

AVRO JETLINER
THE OTHER FIRST JET

The Avro Jetliner first flew in August 1949, and missed its chance to corner the short- to medium-haul civilian turbine market. Only one prototype flew and it was scrapped seven years later. (Jon Proctor Collection)

The world of aeronautical advances is littered with unrequited aircraft and ideas which all share one aspect in common: they are the perfect machines for their moments, but seemingly unexplainably, are never allowed to come to fruition and flourish. The Avro Canada C-102 Jetliner is perhaps the most notable and melancholy of these superb aircraft underachievements.

In the new post-World War II world of 1946, Sir Roy Dobson of A. V. Roe Aircraft in the United Kingdom had a vision of England's Commonwealth partner Canada becoming a leader in the world of aeronautics astride the North American continent. He pledged assistance and financing to the Canadian Victory Aircraft Company, who manufactured Avro aircraft under license for the war. The firm was to be *of* Canada and *for* Canada. One of the first leading-edge projects envisioned was an intercity small- and medium-range jetliner tailored, of course, to the specifications of the nation's leading carrier, Trans-Canada Air Lines (TCA).

The original specifications called for a payload of 32 passengers, with power supplied by two Rolls-Royce axial-flow turbojet engines. However, since Rolls would not release the engine (which subsequently became the Avon) in 1949, Avro was forced to utilize four lower-thrust Derwent centrifugal-flow engines in their final design. What Avro came up with was an outstanding airplane which met or exceeded every one of TCA's many requirements, promising a safe, simple, and reliable airliner for medium-range work. Passenger carriage was up, as was range and performance, and the Jetliner was really becoming something special.

Being not much more than a DC-3 size airline at the time, and following the planning negotiations with Avro, it did not take long for TCA to realize it was in over its head with the Jetliner. They made it clear through many obfuscating excuses that they did not want to be the first airline in North America to fly jets, that responsibility being a bit too much for the line. Unfortunately, political considerations from Ottawa and the powerful Minster C. D. Howe, Minister of Trade (Minister of Everything, as Canadian wags called him) insisted upon keeping Trans-Canada Air Lines as an advisor to the project, and a public pronouncer on the quality of the airplane. It was an airplane they neither wanted, nor wanted promoted, and this was just the beginning of the many sad ironies for the Jetliner.

Now that TCA was no longer the dictating force for the design of the Jetliner, Avro was finally set free to approach U.S. and European airlines. Meanwhile, the prototype aircraft had been taking shape in Malton and made its first flight on August 10, 1949. This date was a mere two weeks after the de Havilland Comet 1 made its maiden flight as the world's first jet-powered airliner. It seemed then that the UK and Commonwealth partners were about to steal a march on the world's airlines.

The Jetliner now could carry 40 to 50 passengers, and flight testing showed the airplane could cruise at 450 mph. The Jetliner made the rounds with the North American airlines, and the first bite for an order came from National in July 1950 and its bigger-than-life president, Ted Baker. From American Airlines engineer to Avro employee came Dixon Speas, so enamored of the Jetliner that he became Avro's U.S. sales representative. Speas lit the fuse on the skyrocket that was Jetliner sales.

When all was said and done, the tally looked like 30 airplanes for the following carriers: National (10) and TWA (20). American, United, Swissair, and Scandinavian Airlines (SAS) were strongly leaning in the same direction. Surprisingly, the U.S. Air Force also decided it liked the Jetliner for navigator and bombardier training and perhaps aerial refueling, and was placing an order for 20 of the jets. As Jim Floyd, the project engineer for the Jetliner said in his wonderful book on the airplane, "The world was Avro's oyster."

Not happy with this tremendous success, C. D. Howe asserted himself into the process once again and forced Avro to stop working on the C-102, favoring shop space being utilized for the CF-100 interceptor. The Korean War theoretically influenced his decision, as did the size of the order from Avro's largest customer, the Canadian government.

Howard Hughes posed for fellow aviator Don Rogers in front of the Avro Jetliner at the Hughes Culver City, California, airfield in April 1952. This is reportedly the only color photograph ever taken of the camera-shy recluse. Captain Rogers was Avro Canada's chief test pilot. (Don Rogers via Bill Mellberg)

Jim Floyd, however, felt that Avro could have indeed managed both the Jetliner and CF-100 programs, but such was not the case. Enter now one Howard Hughes.

One cannot overstate the role Howard Hughes played in nearly resurrecting the C-102. Hughes loved the Jetliner and wanted TWA to fly 20 to 30 of the airplanes on its routes. He worked with Convair in San Diego to license build the airplane for all customers, which meant TWA would have received their first aircraft in May 1954 (equipped with either Allison J33 or Pratt & Whitney J42 engines). The U.S. government quashed the idea after much wrangling with Hughes and Avro, disallowing Convair from utilizing any factory space for production, since the company was ramping-up for its own new interceptor program, the delta wing F-102.

Hughes then told Avro that he would personally finance the building of the airplane *in Canada* if Avro could arrange the space. When Howe discovered this, he was furious, and said "no!" in no uncertain terms. The entrepreneurial approach and gutsy leading-edge leadership of an American visionary was the last chance for the Jetliner, and all that was now extinguished by a single bureaucrat who had nothing but antipathy from the near beginning for this wonderful airplane. After seven years of development, the Jetliner was officially dead.

Operating as a camera ship and chase aircraft for other Avro projects, the Jetliner flew on until November 1956 when time and lack of spare parts caught up with it, and the order was given to scrap the airframe. (The number two aircraft was also destroyed, having never flown and reaching only half completion when the stop order came.)

How much history Avro made with their Jetliner! An excellent airplane for the times, the C-102 could really have put Canada on the map of world-class leaders in aviation production and development. Don't forget that it was this same firm that only a few years later designed the futuristic delta twinjet CF-105 Arrow fighter/interceptor. Continuing the cruel fate of government intervention, Avro also saw that magnificent airplane killed just as it was proving its pedigree. It seems that free markets just didn't matter to the Canadian government in the 1950s, much to the detriment of air forces, airlines, and passengers worldwide.

The transition from props to jets was tumultuous in the early fifties. But had there been an Avro Jetliner fleet plying the routes of America's and Europe's airlines in dependable comfort in those transformative days, that transition would have occurred much faster and more effortlessly than it later did, with commerce and economic growth exploding nearly half a decade earlier. Now *that* would have been quite a world!

Another carrier to operate a substantial DC-4 fleet was Northwest, with 44 of the type. Two from its inventory are seen here at Chicago-Midway, along with a Boeing Stratocruiser, in this classic 1956 photo. Note the boarding steps in the foreground, borrowed from TWA. (Harry Sievers Collection)

Chapter Two

THE JET AGE BEGINS, OR DOES IT?
(1949-1952)

Canyon Starliner, a TWA Lockheed 749A Constellation in 1948. (Craig Kodera/The Greenwich Workshop)

Ever the pioneering country in aviation circles, Great Britain launches an exciting new era in commercial aviation with the world's first turbojet-powered airliner, the magnificent de Havilland Comet. With this gleaming new mode of transportation, the future of air transport was in good hands. Unfortunately, fate and technology intervened, and triumph turned to tragedy in less than two years.

BOAC Comet 1: From Triumph to Tragedy

The riches-to-rags story of Britain's de Havilland Comet 1 has been told countless times. A sleek new airliner powered by turbojet engines is unveiled to an expectant industry in England in 1949. By the summer of 1952, this acclaimed new jetliner is in passenger service on routes throughout Europe and Africa, and a postwar world exults in wonderment at this new technological breakthrough. The joy is short-lived, however, when in January 1954, a Comet 1 disintegrates in midair after taking off from Rome and plunges into the Mediterranean Sea with the loss of all passengers and crew.

Before a curious and grieving world can even understand what happened, a second Comet 1 crashes three months later also after taking off from Rome and under the same mysterious circumstances with the loss of all on board. This was the fifth crash of a Comet in its first two years of commercial operation, and now the race is on to find the technical culprit that is destroying Britain's newest, most modern, and most celebrated airplane. With the second inflight breakup accident comes the immediate grounding of the type, and a loss of face and confidence in Britain's aviation supremacy. What

kind of insidious inflight occurrence caused two of the world's most modern jet aircraft to experience catastrophic structural failure and literally explode in midair? Was it a bomb? Was it human error? Or was it possibly a design flaw in the aircraft itself?

After complex underwater salvage operations aided by the Royal Navy recovered major portions of the airframes from both Rome crashes, the Royal Aircraft Establishment (RAE) at Farnborough launched an investigation of never-before-seen proportions. The hunt began for the cause of the accidents with the reconstruction of actual aircraft wreckage on an armature that indicated beyond any shadow of a doubt the airplane had indeed disintegrated in midair. Then an Italian fisherman's net yielded the "smoking gun" that confirmed the solution to the mystery. A frame from one of the Comet's square passenger windows found in the fisherman's net showed that the fuselage had ruptured from metal fatigue at a point near the corner of the window, extending upward to an equally rectangular Automatic Direction Finder (ADF) antenna housing on the top of the fuselage. The rupture caused an explosive decompression of the cabin, leading to immediate catastrophic structural failure of the rest of the airframe.

Rare art image of the elegant de Havilland Comet 1 in BOAC livery. (Mike Machat Collection)

In historical hindsight, this fact would seem to indicate that de Havilland had not tested its new airplane sufficiently, but nothing could be further from the truth. Knowing full well this airliner would be operating at speeds and altitudes twice that of existing piston-powered aircraft, de Havilland engineers proceeded with fatigue testing of every minute facet of the Comet's design and construction. With untiring effort, structures were put to the test where engineers attempted to duplicate the rigors of countless aircraft "cycles," that is the series of structural loads resulting from a takeoff, climb to altitude, descent from altitude, and landing. Exhaustive testing at Hatfield simulated an aircraft service ceiling of 40,000 feet. What couldn't be duplicated, however, were the severe temperature differentials from sea level to 40,000 feet, and as a result of these accidents, new methods of load simulation were devised at Farnborough for use on future aircraft designs.

With a complete Comet fuselage immersed in a giant tank of water to simulate pressurization forces on the cabin at altitude, patterns now began to emerge that led to the possibility of metal fatigue in the outer skin of the fuselage. When the test cabin itself ruptured inside the water tank, the pattern of metal fatigue was conclusively established. Further study and matching of wreckage fragments from the first Comet lost revealed that the explosive decompression forces were so great that dark blue-black paint from the letter "C" in the BOAC title above the windows was found in a deep gouge on the leading edge of the right wing indicating violent span-wise or lateral impact. This clue graphically showed that the explosive force of the rupture was so great that it exceeded the forward velocity of the airplane at that moment.

As with any aviation accident, tragedy yields information and knowledge so that a particular problem can be avoided in the future. In the case of the Comet, metallurgy techniques, manufacturing methodology, and aircraft skin structural properties were modified to include an integral reinforcing framework built into the skin itself much like "quilted" aluminum foil used in common households today. Additionally, the passenger windows on all British airliners built after these accidents were manufactured in the shape of an ovaloid to eliminate the smaller-radius corners from which the fatal fatigue cracks emanated on both Comets that disintegrated.

Although the reputation of Britain's commercial aviation industry was tarnished by the discovery of the design flaw that led to these accidents, de Havilland went back to the drawing board and developed improved and more advanced versions of the Comet which eventually reentered passenger service in 1958 and flew successfully well into the latter part of the twentieth century. But the story of the Comet deserves closer scrutiny than just the crash investigation, as this airplane represented the great hope and rebirth of Europe's proud aviation industry rising from the ashes of World War II's destruction, and was intended to show the world that England was once again a leader in aircraft design.

Evolving from design studies in 1944 for a small jet-powered mail airplane with a canard wing planform, the original de Havilland Comet was envisioned as a small high-speed, six-passenger transport powered by three turbojets buried in the aircraft's tail section. As further marketing studies clearly indicated the need for a larger-capacity aircraft, the DH-106 emerged as the final configuration, featuring four 5,000-pound-thrust de Havilland Ghost turbojet engines buried inside the wing root with a slightly swept wing and conventional straight tailplanes. This new aircraft would carry 44 passengers at speeds of 490 mph on route segments of up to 1,500 miles. With its bare metal skin gleaming in the hazy summer sunshine, the formerly secret jetliner was rolled out of the factory hangar on July 27, 1949.

First flown at Hatfield later that very same day by de Havilland's Chief Test Pilot, John Cunningham, the Comet wowed all observers although most of the crowd, including the British Press, had already gone

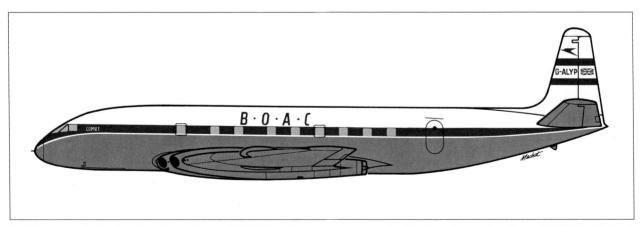

Profile artwork depicts the classic lines of BOAC's color scheme as applied to the pioneering Comet 1. (Mike Machat)

home thinking the flight would be scrubbed due to typically inclement British weather. As word spread of this new airplane's successful and impressive flight trials, the traveling public began to anticipate a sense of futurism at the thought of being able to actually fly around the world in a jet-powered commercial airliner. Such an expectation was especially pervasive considering that only the Canadians had a competing design with their smaller Avro Jetliner, and that the American aviation industry didn't even have an airplane on the drawing boards to seriously compete for the Comet's pride of place.

Ordered initially by BOAC, the Comet 1 soon began to attract the attention of other world airlines, and tentative orders followed from Aeromaritime, Air France, Canadian Pacific, the Royal Canadian Air Force, and Britain's Royal Air Force. With the promise of even larger and longer-range Comet versions, Pan American World Airways and Capital Airlines in the United States proudly added their names to de Havilland's order book. By the time BOAC's first Comet 1 entered passenger service on the London–South Africa route on May 2, 1952 (via Rome, Cairo, and points south), the airplane was firmly expected to be a world beater, bringing deluxe passen-

ger service and significantly reduced travel times to routes emanating from Europe, and eventually other continents as well.

To put the Comet's operational service into perspective, simply read about the other airliners flying at this same time. In 1954, Lockheed Constellations along with the Douglas DC-6 and DC-7 were the pressurized "queens of the skies" throughout the world, offering new levels of passenger comfort, speed, and range to the world's airlines. This was especially true when compared to the unpressurized 200-mph Douglas DC-4s that entered service immediately following the war. With the Comet, the world had a brand-new airliner capable of more than doubling all of these operational parameters in the same time period.

By the beginning of 1954, BOAC's Comet routes had expanded to include the Middle East, India, Singapore, and Japan. As was inevitable with any new paradigm, however, accidents began to occur that, in all fairness, could have happened with any aircraft. On October 26, 1952, a Comet was damaged after stalling on takeoff in Rome. On March 2, 1953, another Comet was destroyed while taking off from Karachi, and then on May 2, 1953, a third Comet was lost in a raging thunderstorm near Calcutta. These accidents did not go

Good intentions but false hopes are represented in this photo of a model of the advanced Comet III ordered by Pan American World Airways. The new jet was expected to enter Pan Am service in 1956, but became eclipsed by the development of larger and faster American jetliners following the Comet 1 accidents. (Craig Kodera Collection)

unnoticed, but when Comet G-ALYP mysteriously fell from the sky near Alba, Italy, on January 10, 1954, the world took special notice. BOAC temporarily grounded all of its Comets until it was determined that what had occurred was strictly a one-time happenstance, and the type was returned to service on March 23. Then, only two weeks later on April 8, Comet G-ALYY repeated the Alba tragedy, and the Comet 1's brief but supreme reign was over.

Aircraft of the Era

Progress in aeronautics is nothing if not fast. Starting in the mid-1930s, commercial aircraft design took a huge leap skyward with the first DC-2 and DC-3, which at the time were termed the "Giant Douglas Flagships" by American Airlines. These twin-engine airliners were soon eclipsed by the four-engine Douglas DC-4E and Boeing 307, followed by the production DC-4 and Lockheed Constellation, with the Douglas DC-6 being considered the thoroughbred of that era. This significant march forward spanned a total of only 12 years, and took us from airplanes carrying 21 passengers in sometimes grueling unpressurized multi-stop transcontinental service, all the way to luxurious skyliners carrying 50 passengers in pressurized comfort spanning the great oceans, and doing so at about twice the speed of the fastest aircraft a decade earlier. Even at the intercity level, the modern new "twins" from Convair and Martin enjoyed the same speed and habitable higher-altitude cabins as the larger aircraft. We see that the world of postwar commercial aviation enjoyed a quantum improvement from its pioneering forebears of the Depression era.

Lockheed Constellation 049 through 149

It is easy to lose sight of the fact that what started in 1936, as the modest 36-passenger Excalibur airliner from Lockheed, became the 049 Constellation only three years later, which was an airplane with a pressurized cabin capable of carrying 46 passengers over a distance of 3,500 miles. At TWA's behest for nine orders, Lockheed commenced with the airplane, making it the company's largest undertaking to date. Pan American ordered 40 of the transoceanic type 149 (decreased in 1945 due to an order for the Boeing Stratocruiser). The prototype Constellation made its first flight on January 9, 1943, smack in the middle of the war. The airplane wore standard olive-drab-and-gray USAAF camouflage and insignia. This date highlights the reason that the very advanced Constellation became available to the airlines so soon after the war. The first Constellations were actually Army Air Force C-69 transports, and prior to the war's end, Lockheed manufactured 31 of these airframes making them available to the airlines at incredibly low prices.

High speed for the Constellation was derived from its powerful Curtiss-Wright R-3350 Duplex Cyclone engines, which gave the aircraft a 25-percent boost in power versus the Douglas DC-4. The "Connie," as the flying public knew it, also offered greater range, faster speed, higher payload capability, and a commensurate lowering of cost-per-seat-mile [the cost of moving one passenger seat over a distance of one mile] some 23 percent below the Douglas airliner. (Note: This book chronicles the ongoing and ever-present crosstown rivalry and "back and forth" success between the designs of Lockheed and Douglas during the 1940s and 1950s. There always seemed to

Despite the rapid delivery of DC-6s, United Air Lines continued to operate well-maintained but older DC-4s for several years. Mainliner Yellowstone, pictured at Oakland, California, in 1952, looks smart in the carrier's new white crown livery. (William T. Larkins)

Inflight portrait of the Lockheed 049 Constellation shows the classic lines of the big Connie, triple tail and all. The outer-wing planform borrowed heavily from the lines of Lockheed's twin-tail World War II fighter, the P-38 Lightning. (TWA/Jon Proctor Collection)

The "front office" of an early-model Constellation shows cockpit state of the art, circa late 1940s. Note fabric-covered alcohol pans above the pilot and co-pilot glare shields that were used for de-icing the inner panes of the aircraft's windshield. Although appearing rather primitive by today's standards, this cockpit was considered just as advanced in its day as GPS navigation and digital instrumentation are now. (Craig Kodera Collection)

be a competition for orders between these two Southern California airliner giants.) The 049 was also the first production transport to have hydraulically boosted controls.

Pan American began the first scheduled transatlantic service via the Constellation on January 20, 1946, from New York to Lisbon, while the first transcontinental service came from TWA on February 15, 1946. TWA offered one-stop service between Los Angeles and New York for a scheduled time of 9 hours 45 minutes. This was in stark contrast to United's and American's unpressurized DC-4s that made two stops while crossing the United States. This advantage made TWA the leader in postwar transcontinental service, although that would dissipate one year later as the DC-6 began its work at American and United.

Douglas DC-6

Beginning in 1944, designers at Douglas Aircraft in Santa Monica were working toward a stretched and pressurized improvement of their then-current DC-4/C-54. The key to this stretch was the Pratt & Whitney R-2800 Double Wasp engine. As we saw above with the Constellation, and indeed as would be seen for the decades following this time period, engine advancement and the proper mating with the appropriate airframe would literally make or break an aeronautical design.

The DC-6 (later known as "the straight-6") incorporated many firsts for an airliner, and learned lessons from the first Constellations, thus refining the air travel "product" even further. For instance, the DC-6 had the first cabin heated by radiant heat in the cabin walls and floor; no-fog passenger windows; electric de-icing of

A United Douglas DC-6 taxies by the camera wearing the airline's new "white crown" color scheme with revised markings. The upper fuselage was painted white to reflect sunlight and maintain lower temperatures inside the cabin when the aircraft was parked on the ground. (Craig Kodera Collection)

Wearing the airline's famous "Airline of the Stars" motto, a National DC-6 is seen about to start engines at Philadelphia in 1957. (Harry Sievers)

the wings, tail, and propellers; it was the first airliner to be air conditioned both in the air and on the ground; and it featured a cabin, which was pressurized automatically depending on altitude. The DC-6 boasted that a selected cabin temperature could be maintained within 3 degrees Fahrenheit because of the advanced heating/air conditioning in the airplane.

One competitive aspect of the DC-6/Constellation duel was each airplane's fuselage design. Lockheed created a beautiful and aerodynamically inspired curvaceous body for its airliner, and claimed lower drag and higher speeds (with a slight addition in lift). Douglas continued with its utilitarian approach to cabin design, and because it chose a cylindrical "tube" for its airplane, realized far more capability in terms of space and its utilization. It could also be argued that a constant-section cylinder is easier to adapt to a stretch and, therefore, easier to expand upon to grow the airframe (which we will indeed witness later). It is subjective, of course; we believe the early cabin interiors of the Douglas airplane had a more luxurious feel to them versus the Constellation, due to the use of a constant-diameter fuselage and cabin.

The DC-6 began life much like the 049: as a transport for the military services. The assigned number for the design was YC-112A. It flew for the first time on February 15, 1946 (a year after the Constellation entered airline service), and began flying in commercial service for American Airlines on April 27, 1947. This was also the day when United Airlines inaugurated its own DC-6 service. American had ordered 50 of the airplanes, United 35. American's aircraft had accommodations for sleeper berths and the telltale small berth windows at the top of the fuselage. American's configuration was fifty passengers by day, or 24 by night using the berths.

As noted, the previous competitive edge enjoyed by TWA and its Constellations had, by September 1947, been replaced by the tripartite division of traffic across the United States that was pretty much in place prior to the war. The breakdown was as follows: American Airlines, 47 percent; TWA, 37 percent; and United Airlines, 16 percent.

A total of 175 DC-6s were built by Douglas before production ended in 1951.

A California intrastate carrier at the time, Pacific Southwest Airlines acquired four DC-4s from Capital in the mid-1950s and saved money by retaining much of Capital's livery, including square outlines around the oval windows to give the impression of a more-modern and fully pressurized DC-6. N30068, a converted military C-54, appears ready for departure at San Francisco in October 1957. (Harry Sievers)

Lockheed Constellation 649 through 749

By May 1945, Lockheed had begun updating the basic Constellation design, with a weight increase as the number-one attribute of this "new" airplane. Over the ensuing years Lockheed basically pioneered the use of step-increases in overall weight capabilities, thus allowing expanded roles for the airframe in a larger market. Through the redesign effort the "new type" Constellation, as Eastern Airlines referred to it (649/749), was actually a 50-percent-change baseline airplane. Now that the Wright 3350 "BD-1" version of the engine was available at 300 bhp more than the original installed in the 049s, the airplane could be enhanced noticeably. Faster airspeed and greater payload performance, plus better inside soundproofing (to match the DC-6), better heating, ventilation, and cooling set the new-series Constellations apart from the originals.

One of the more interesting aspects to the added utility of the 649/749 series was the use of an external cargo-carrying pod, which was slung under the centerline of the fuselage at mid-wing. This was known as the "Speedpak" and could carry 8,000 pounds of additional cargo. Lockheed sold 75 Speedpaks, mainly to Eastern, KLM (Royal Dutch Airlines), and TWA, for use on 049, 649, and 749 airframes. (As an aside, Eastern paid $850,000 for each 649 it purchased—quite a hefty amount in 1948!)

The first of the 749s went to Air France in April 1947. The 749 had additional 565-gallon fuel tanks installed in the outboard wings, which increased its range by 1,000 miles while allowing it to carry the same payload as the 649. This was the overwater version of the Constellation that became the gold standard of the short bodies, which allowed it to find wide acceptance with far-flung overseas airlines such as BOAC, Qantas, and South African. The 749/749A was also the model of the Constellation that remained in service the longest, on routes both around the world and in the United States.

The favorite Constellation model among pilots was the 749A. With greater fuel capacity, increased maximum takeoff weight, and other improvements, it could routinely fly nonstop from New York to northern European destinations. (TWA/Jon Proctor Collection)

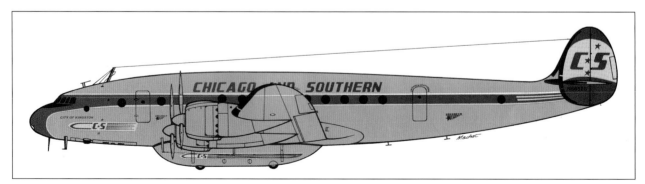

This profile view shows the aerodynamically designed Speedpak external cargo carrier to best advantage. Note the semi-retracted wheels at each corner of the novel device for ease in ground handling. (Mike Machat)

Air France also provided its passengers flying between Paris and New York the unique Golden Parisian service on 749 sleeper aircraft. The usual 24-passenger sleeper seating eventually gave way to a 16-passenger layout, which provided the kind of legroom one could only find on a ship, or in one's own living room! Such was intercontinental air travel during the early postwar years.

Hostess Lynne Stanton serves breakfast in bed to a passenger riding TWA's deluxe Ambassador sleeper flight across the Atlantic. (TWA/Jon Proctor Collection)

A cocktail lounge located at the front of the 749A Constellation passenger cabin provided a casual atmosphere for passengers awaiting dinner, or makeup of their sleeping berths, on TWA's nonstop Ambassador Service from New York to London. Purser Russ Robins and a hostess prepare to offer champagne to their guests. (TWA/Jon Proctor Collection)

THE VISIONARIES

Throughout the Industrial Revolution in America, bold, farsighted men carved out a country that flourished beyond their wildest expectations. Midway into the period of American exceptionalism, the fledgling airline industry required, and acquired, men such as those who preceded them: huge dreamers, bold and decisive leaders, the inspirational creators of an entirely new system of transportation. These were the men who didn't just lead but "became" their own airline companies, and by doing so, gave the world wings. Below are three of many; perhaps *the* three most influential airline presidents who shepherded into the modern era the airlines they so proudly ran.

W. A. "Pat" Patterson, United

Plucked from Wells Fargo Bank, after being the loan officer in charge of the Pacific Air Transport (PAT) account, William A. "Pat" Patterson was hired by Boeing Air Transport after it bought PAT in 1929. He was placed in the company as general manager under its president at that time, Philip Johnson. Soon thereafter, the presidency became his. Patterson's tenure at what became United Airlines lasted some 32 years, and at the time of his retirement, United Air Lines was the largest airline in the free world.

Pat Patterson ran United as a very hands-on manager, usually spending one third of his year traveling the routes of the airline so as to keep an eye on its functioning and to meet the employees. He was a legend when it came to remembering names. His administration was one of shared commitment, and he stressed five rules to utilize in everyday airline work life. They were (in order of importance) safety, passenger comfort, dependability, honesty, and sincerity.

Perhaps the biggest early decision Patterson made was in response to the San Francisco Traffic Manager's suggestion that the airline utilize nurses onboard the airplanes in order to care for the needs of the passengers. Eight young women were hired and became the world's first professional stewardesses.

Under his watchful eye, other firsts at United included: the first airborne kitchen for inflight meals; the first nighttime scheduled services for coast-to-coast and long-distance routes; and two-way radio communications. This last point also bears on the fact that United had a radio laboratory that also investigated other aspects of advancing flight and aerial nav-

United Chairman William A. Patterson was a close friend of Donald Douglas, and was known to order airplanes from "Doug" just by picking up the phone. United flew every major Douglas type, and was a launch customer for several Douglas airliners including the DC-8. (Jon Proctor Collection)

igation. Additionally, United had a lead role in creating special airfare promotions like taking your wife along for free on your business trip, and men only "executive" service (see Chapter 8 sidebar, "United's Magnificent Caravelle," page 122). United also helped refine and then launch the Douglas DC-8 Jetliner.

C. R. Smith, American

Another financial whiz kid, Cyrus Rowlett Smith, or Mr. C.R., or just "C.R.," was an imposing figure of a man, standing just over six-foot-one-inch tall. A compassionate yet sometimes gruff manager, Smith got things done at American, even though he originally had no interest in running an airline. Once

American Airlines' guiding light throughout the 1930s, 1940s, and 1950s was Cyrus R. Smith, who understood the profound impact air travel would have on National commerce as well as the traveling public. (Craig Kodera Collection)

Pioneering "firsts" in the airline industry under C.R. included: first national campaign to sell seats; first credit purchase program; first passenger lounges (Admirals' Clubs); first airline service into LaGuardia Airport (thus assuring American's overwhelming presence), first transcontinental jet service; first stewardess college; and the first airline to carry one million passengers during a year (1937). American also helped pioneer the VOR (Visual Omni Range) system of navigation, today's staple. It caused the launch of many significant airliners including the Convair 240 and 990; the Lockheed Electra (see Chapter 4); and the Douglas DC-6, DC-7, and DC-10.

As impressive as these achievements may have been, perhaps the most significant action ever taken by C.R. Smith was his insistence, during a marathon two-hour phone call, that Don Douglas build a larger DC-2 derivative called the Douglas Sleeper Transport, which became better known as the DC-3. From that point on, the world of transport aviation was never the same, and by 1936, airlines were finally showing a profit carrying only passengers, and not having to depend on U.S. Mail contracts.

Juan Trippe, Pan American

A Yale graduate, Juan Terry Trippe was always thinking of aviation. His first venture was Long Island Airways from 1923 to 1925, and then The Aviation Corporation of America. In what would become his hallmark operating style, Trippe became a manager of mergers, appending one airline after another to the core airline (which in 1931 officially became Pan American Airways). That airline started in the Caribbean, then expanded into Mexico, then South America, Latin America, the Atlantic, and finally China and the Pacific. Often thought of as "determined," Trippe also had a reputation for sometimes being a bit unethical. However, the end results always favored *his* airline, Pan American.

Juan Trippe was a very patient man. If he wanted something he'd be willing to wait to get it but all the while wearing down his intended target until finally, he or they gave in. Trippe also learned early-on how to work within the system, a necessity since overseas route authority was granted by the government. Trippe's influence was a constantly growing entity, and his vision for his airline was that of the sole U.S. Flag Carrier, or "The Chosen Instrument" to project America's greatness. But no matter how he achieved his goals, Pan American was indeed the undisputed premier international airline in the world.

selected for the job of running Texas Air Transport, he threw himself into the occupation, going so far as to get his pilot's license. Once in charge of the entire amalgamated airline after 1934, C.R. made aviation history time and again through American Airlines. He was president from 1934 until 1968.

C.R. was what we call today a workaholic manager, always flying the line and tweaking American's service and its business. He usually flew anonymously, and on standby at that, with a similar penchant as Patterson for remembering employee's names and family details. It wasn't surprising to see a short letter from C.R. noting a good, or bad, occasion. It was a small aviation world back then.

One indicator of his bravura was the launching of the national ad campaign boldly asking if the average person was afraid to fly. This was the unspoken reality of commercial aviation in the 1920s and 1930s, and C.R. brought it into the open and pointed out that American's number-one priority was safe transportation in the air. By the end of the 1930s, American was carrying one third of all U.S. airline passengers.

Pan American World Airways Chairman Juan T. Trippe was a fierce competitor, but also a shrewd businessman when it came to international air transportation. Father of the Flying Clippers, Trippe guided Pan Am as the premier international flag carrier of the United States. (Mike Machat Collection)

Pan American Airways flew to most of its destinations as the *first* airline ever to do so. When one is the pioneer, one quickly learns that everything must be built from scratch. The airline was renowned for its engineering prowess, and its navigational equipment was the leader in its field. Becoming and maintaining a rating as a Pan American airline pilot or navigator (pilots had to be proficient at both jobs) was governed by the strictest of standards and proficiency levels. Pan American was able to strike out into completely uncharted territory and build by hand a transoceanic airline, its 1935 Transpacific island service being the prime example. (Remember always the beautiful China Clippers and their siblings.)

Pan American was an airline of firsts too numerous to mention here; suffice it to say that when one thinks of the romance and intrigue of girdling the planet in an airplane in those early days, and taking two weeks to do so, only one airline name comes to mind: Pan American World Airways. Among his countless accomplishments, Juan Trippe would also have to be considered "the father of the modern jet airliner," placing the historic launch order for Boeing's new 707 in 1955, and then again in 1966 for the world's first Jumbo Jet, the Boeing 747. Juan Trippe retired as CEO in 1968 and left the board in 1975. He guided and shaped his beloved and historic company for nearly half a century, and what a half century it was!

Convair 240

While DC-3s had served the airlines well since the mid-1930s, the type was considered slow and flew through more bad weather than it could climb over. Airline managers wanted a new twin-engine, short- to medium-range replacement with added capacity, more speed, and a pressurized cabin.

At San Diego, the Consolidated Vultee Aircraft Corporation, recognized as "Convair," first flew its prototype Model 110 on July 8, 1946. From this 30-seat variant, the production Model 240 was developed, gaining its name from the *two*-engine, *40*-passenger configuration. It featured a tricycle landing gear along with the pressurized cabin and added speed desired by the airlines. The 240 prototype first flew on March 16, 1947.

Designed for short-haul, multi-stop route segments, the 240 design offered optional self-contained airstairs and claimed a maximum speed of 300 mph, although 275 mph was a more realistic cruising speed for day-to-day operations. Its list price was $495,000, a far cry from the $10,000 cost of a surplus C-47 after the war.

Convair factory artist's rendering of the interior for Convair's new Model 240 twin-engine transport showing passenger seats, galley, lavatory, and baggage stowage. It does seem odd, however, that the airplane is shown in flight, complete with exhaust-thrust augmentation from the engines, yet with no people aboard. (Craig Kodera Collection)

Built by Consolidated Vultee Aircraft Corporation, the prototype Convair Model 110 flew for the first time on July 8, 1946, lifting off from San Diego's Lindbergh Field. This planned 30-seat airliner design gave way to the popular Convair 240 that first flew less than a year later. (Consolidated Vultee/Jon Proctor Collection)

American Airlines became the Convair-Liner launch customer with a massive order for 100 Model 240s to replace its workhorse DC-3s and provide further route expansion. The Convairs provided short-haul service to destinations such as Roanoke, Virginia, where Flagship Algonquin was headed from New York's LaGuardia Airport. (Allan Van Wickler)

The type's production had been assured in 1945 by an American Airlines order for 100 airplanes (later lowered to 75), purchased to replace the carrier's DC-3 fleet and provide further route expansion. It also had the advantage of Pratt & Whitney R-2800 engines, common with American's planned four-engine Douglas DC-6 fleet. Convairs began flying for the airline on June 1, 1948.

Another 13 airlines bought 240s. The DC-3s they replaced were gradually sold off, many to the newly designated U.S. local service carriers. Convair produced 176 Model 240s, including two built in executive configurations. The success of the program was enriched by production of 390 military variants produced in five different configurations for the U.S. Air Force and U.S. Navy.

The Martinliners

The Baltimore, Maryland–based Glenn L. Martin Company first flew its Model 202 four months after the Convair 240 and launched the type with orders for 35 airplanes. The 40-seat variant was not pressurized and suffered from design problems early on. However, the first 202 entered service with Northwest Airlines in October 1947, eight months ahead of the Convair 240's debut with American Airlines. Utilizing Pratt & Whitney R-2800 engines, the 202 claimed a maximum speed of slightly more than 300 mph, and cruised at 277 mph.

Despite an early order book that at one time totaled 270 airplanes, the 202s found a home in large numbers with just one U.S. carrier (Northwest); only six more airframes were purchased, split between two South

American carriers, Linea Aérea National (LAN-Chile) and Linea Aéropostal Venezolana (LAV). Northwest, the only major 202 purchaser, almost immediately removed four seats from the airplanes to eliminate problems with insufficient galley and carry-on luggage space. A fatal accident caused by wing failure, along with four unrelated accidents and the subsequent refusal of Northwest's pilots to fly the type, was cause for the airline to ground its Martin fleet in March 1951. Eight airplanes were sold and the remaining 12 leased to other operators.

A pressurized 202 version, the Model 303, was launched to better compete with the Convair 240. But redesign and production delays prompted customers, including United Air Lines, to cancel orders; the program was shelved in October 1947, even after two prototypes were built.

Martin instead chose to press ahead with the further-improved Model 404 that would comfortably seat 40, thanks to a 39-inch fuselage stretch. Uprated R-2800-CB-16 engines and an improved landing gear design made the 404 a more competitive product against Convair's new twin, and the 404 cruised at 280 mph with a top speed of 312 mph.

Eastern Air Lines and TWA became the 404 launch customers with large orders after Convair declined a request to improve the 240 design. In 1950, TWA agreed to buy 30 new 404s (10 more were ordered 16 months later). It then leased and later purchased 12 uncompleted 202s after Martin offered modifications to bring them up to an improved "202A" standard, and began receiving the type in July.

Eastern, which had earlier canceled its 202 order, signed up for the 404 with a contract for 35, later boosting the total to 60 airplanes. Both carriers placed the type into service in December 1951. As with the Convairs, the new Martins replaced DC-3s and even TWA's five Boeing 307 Stratoliners in feederline service.

Despite the best efforts of Martin's salesmen, the 404 only attracted the two launch orders. Howard

While waiting for delivery of its Martin 404s, TWA leased a dozen 202A models that had sat unsold at the manufacturer's Baltimore plant, and later bought these twelve airplanes to support its expanding traffic and routes. (TWA/Jon Proctor Collection)

Eastern Airlines Martin 404 Silver Falcon in flight. (Craig Kodera Collection)

Hughes coupled the contract for TWA with one airframe for his personal use, and two RM-1 military variants. The last two airplanes off the assembly line went to the U.S. Coast Guard.

Produced in greater numbers than the 202, Martin's 404s found second careers with several airlines and corporate operators, mainly in the United States.

Safety and Reliability—Not Quite There Yet

Perhaps the greatest impediment to the widespread acceptance of air travel as the key mode of transportation in this country, and around the world for that matter, was the ever-present perception of the danger of flying. During the 1920s and 1930s, survival in air transportation was almost akin to living in the Wild West of the nineteenth century, comparable to traversing the country in covered wagons through Indian territory. Airliner crashes became constant newsreel fodder, and mothers begged their sons to take the train and not fly. The Fokker Trimotor or Curtiss Condor seemed like lumbering box kites just waiting to be swatted out of the sky by a fierce storm.

However, each successive decade following World War I did indeed manage to see incremental and then quantum advances in aircraft design, and as a consequence, airframe and systems reliability marched steadily forward. Compare the change from the wooden Fokker X to the all-metal Ford Trimotor. It was a wooden-wing spar in a Fokker that broke apart in a thunderstorm killing famed Notre Dame football coach Knute Rockne and galvanizing public sentiment against air travel. It was nothing less than a tectonic shift from the corrugated Ford to the sleek monocoque Boeing 247, and then the grand DC-3 in 1936.

These aircraft brought new standards of flying safety and reliability, but all things remained relative, and airplanes still had a nasty tendency to crash. As discussed later, the airlines of the 1930s were obsessed with advertising campaigns aimed at bolstering the safety of flight and the quality of their product. American Airlines even went so far as to broach the subject of safety in their ads. That frankness seemed to have a positive effect overall, but flying was still not like taking the old, dependable train.

Following World War II, four-engine transports like the Lockheed Constellation and Douglas DC-6, along with the new twins from Convair and Martin, launched the next refinement of the technological base featuring pressurized passenger cabins and strong all-metal construction utilizing new advanced aluminum materials. Augmenting this were radio navigation aids, a flight engineer to handle the new complex technologies, weather mitigating devices such as heated wing and tail leading edges and propeller deicing systems, and of course, the obvious redundancy of two more engines on the larger transports.

And yet, airliners kept running afoul of consistent safety records. Airplanes still crashed often enough to give many folks a fleeting second thought before boarding a "giant silver bird" or "queen of the sky" bound for points near and far. Train service continued to maintain its passenger appeal even throughout the 1950s. So what was causing that persistent, albeit lowered, sense of worry when it came to flying commercially?

The Civil Aeronautics Administration (CAA) mandated that all Low- and Medium-Frequency (LMF) radio ranges be decommissioned in favor of new the technology, Visual Omni Range (VOR). Lighted airways were nearly a relic of the past, leftovers of the airmail open cockpit days. Most major airports were now equipped with Instrument Landing System (ILS) precision approach aids, and en route traffic radar centers popped up across the nation to separate airplanes from one another along the airways. Aircraft were flying higher and avoiding more weather, flying faster to stay ahead of that weather, and flying with greater fuel range

As the airline industry matured and grew, new modern "super airports" came into existence to serve the equally new and modern airliners carrying more and more passengers every year. Here we see a gleaming new LaGuardia Airport terminal and tower with a United DC-3 flying overhead in 1939. The terminal building contained a glamorous restaurant and sweeping observation deck back in the day when a trip to the airport was considered an exciting excursion for the entire family. (Mike Machat Collection)

so as to be able to go around that weather. Advanced weather radar onboard the DC-6B, DC-7 series, and 1049/1649 Constellation series (covered in Chapters 3, 4, and 5, respectively) all added more margins of dependability to daily airline operations. So why were airliners continuing to fall out of the sky?

For all the technology invented to improve piston-powered airplanes, and as the working and regulatory environment for fast aircraft continued to grow (although always seemingly behind the latest speed and efficiency of the airplanes it served), it appeared that two chronic problems kept hampering a better safety record for airliners in the late 1940s and the 1950s: *unreliable* technology and weather.

Piston engines such as the Wright R-3350 Turbo Compound or Pratt & Whitney R-4360 Double Wasp certainly marked the pinnacle of reciprocating power-plant technology and made possible the advancements noted above, but the very complexity of these engines was also their Achilles heel. More complex than a Swiss watch, these engines required as much maintenance per-flight-hour as several fleets of DC-3s combined! They certainly were not reliable. How many DC-7s landed at their destinations with one engine shut down, its propeller feathered? How often did contemporary films characterize airliner engines as being temperamental and cantankerous devices that came apart in flight, threw propellers, and then burned up, terrorizing all passengers onboard?

When one examines hull loss statistics in the United States from 1946 to the present, the overall number of accidents still falls within a pretty narrow range. The negative trend, however, existed in the *types* of hulls destroyed. A striking reality found in the probable cause of each accident in the prop era identifies the aircraft more often than not as a commercial transport. As years pass with the world's airlines fully transitioning to all-jet fleets, the same number of accidents then begins shifting more to general aviation or small regional aircraft. Today, air safety for commercial transports around the world, and especially here in the United States, is enviably exemplary, with more people flying per-airplane, per-day, and on more airlines and airplanes than ever imaginable in the early 1950s.

Although technology has truly made a life-sustaining difference to air travelers today, aviation still suffers the occasional grandiose air accident with its attendant headlines, especially those involving large jetliners with hundreds of passengers aboard. What is the explanation? Many times we still see weather as a culprit, for we just cannot surmount every single type of atmospheric disturbance Mother Nature sends our way. Mighty jet airliners have been ripped apart by thunderstorms, and ice is still the largest operational problem faced by the air transport industry. Let's flash back to earlier times and imagine flying in a Constellation somewhere over the East Coast in February.

The airplane is flying in ice more than in the clear, and because the Connie uses rubber deicer boots on its leading edges, you can actually see the wings icing up, then the boots expanding to break sheets of it loose. It even shears off the prop blades and slams against the fuselage. The weather is abysmal all the way down to a near zero-zero landing and you're landing at a field without an ILS, so the Captain is conducting a VOR, or in really tough situations, an ADF (Automatic Direction Finder) approach.

Landing minimums are higher for these non-precision approaches, which means you may or may not see the ground from those slightly higher altitudes. Hopefully the wind isn't so strong that you are blown completely off course, placing you farther away from your missed approach point, where you either see the runway or have to execute a go-around and try again, or even divert to your landing alternate.

Our pilot has flown into this airport "a million times" and he's sure he knows where he is by looking straight down at the ground. If only he can get a few feet lower and sneak into the clear to be able to see the runway straight ahead. As he gingerly continues to feel for clear air, the copilot suddenly screams, "Pull Up!"

But with engines snarling with increased power to escape impending disaster, the ground rushes up to meet the aircraft, the left wingtip contacts the earth, and the rest of our story becomes tragic front-page news the next morning.

More the exception than the rule, the above scenario focuses again on an inherent complexity, and how this aspect of postwar propliner operational capability affected air safety. Flying a large, piston-engine airliner, already an extremely complex system, within another incredibly complex system (radio navigational aids) while at the mercy of a precocious and unpredictable weather phenomena is just begging for the ominous chain of events found in all air accidents to be forged, several links at a time.

It is, therefore, a vast tribute to the men we called aviators in those days that many a safe trip was concluded at their hands despite all the challenges. By the late 1950s, these incredibly talented and wise individuals began to experience first-hand the almost unbelievable improvement in safety standards, and the simplicity of flight operations made available to the airlines when the world finally transitioned from props to jets.

Chapter Three

PISTONS FOREVER!
(1952-1954)

Puddle Jumper, *an American Airlines Convair 240 in 1954.* (Craig Kodera)

The piston-engine airliner evolves and matures to new and impressive levels, bringing greater speed, longer range, and increased passenger capacity as well as true transcontinental travel. Aircraft performance increases, and so does the level of operational safety and reliability. International air travel also comes of age as airline routes expand and more passengers take to the skies than ever before.

State of the Industry in 1954

By 1954, air travel had permeated the awareness of the general public. No longer only for the rich, traveling aboard a modern airliner was now a concept embraced by more and more of the U.S. and international populace. America's favorite pilot, Arthur Godfrey, loved to talk about the safety and reliability of modern airliners on his TV shows, and it seemed as if every ad for a new car featured a giant silver Constellation flying gracefully overhead. When compared to today's statistics, however, the percentage of people in the United States who had actually experienced flying aboard a commercial airliner in 1954 seems staggeringly low—only three percent, with the noticeable majority of these travelers being businessmen.

Be that as it may, people could now board a DC-7 or Super Constellation and travel across the United States in pressurized comfort at speeds of 300 mph and altitudes in excess of 20,000 feet. For regional or local service, the new and improved Convair 340 would probably be the aircraft of choice. Airlines even structured their routing to combine the best of both worlds; you could fly coast-to-coast in the DC-7 and then connect to your final destination in the Convair. Businessmen flying on regional airlines could now leave on their sales calls or attend that big meeting across the state in the morning, and be home easily in time for dinner that evening.

Vacation travel abroad, although becoming more prevalent by air, was still considered something done more suitably by steamship than by airplane. This was understandable considering the number of elegant new ships taking to the oceans in 1954. The magnificent S.S. *United States* was breaking transatlantic speed records nearly every time she sailed, while the smaller S.S. *Independence* and *Constitution* were equally majestic. Cunard's glorious Art Deco twins, the HMS *Queen Mary* and *Queen Elizabeth* handily proved the adage "Getting there is half the fun!" The brand-new (and ill-fated) Italian *Andrea Doria* and her sister ship *Cristoforo Colombo* looked like floating art museums on the inside. Passengers didn't mind spending the better part of a week getting to Europe from the East Coast (or to Hawaii and Asia from the West Coast) by ship because of the sumptuous level of service.

When the modern propeller-driven airliner is entered into the equation of vacation travel in 1954, we see the factors of pure speed versus luxurious service being prevalent. European cities were 10 or 12 hours away from New York by airplane rather than five or six days by ship; getting there quickly was the clear priority.

Supplemental carrier Transocean Air Lines flew DC-4s to the four corners of the world, both in cargo and passenger configurations, from its Oakland, California, base. TALOA was an acronym for Transocean Air Lines followed by the two-letter Oakland airport code. This operation was the spawning ground for the Ernie Gann story that led to the epic Warner Brothers motion picture, **The High and the Mighty.** (William T. Larkins)

Still, this time period represented the heyday of modern ocean liners, and nothing from commercial aviation could stop it. What would be required to greatly impact oceanic travel was a radical new powerplant that could propel commercial airliners to almost the speed of sound, much like Great Britain had attempted with its pioneering Comet, but with much greater range and larger passenger capacity. Although military aircraft were reaping the benefits of this new powerplant, the reality of 600-mph airliners was still many years away.

The radical new powerplant necessary to take commercial aviation to the next level and eradicate the competition for long-range travel from ocean liners was called, quite simply, the modern turbojet engine.

Jetliners on the Distant Horizon: USAF Enters the Turbine Age

In the 1930s, there existed a dichotomy within the aeronautical engineering world that had a profound effect on future aircraft in the United States and Britain: Civilian airplanes, especially air racers (and those were mostly built by entrepreneurs in small out buildings or garages), were more aerodynamically advanced, mean-

ing faster and more maneuverable, than our frontline fighter aircraft in the military services! This differential had an enormous effect on aircraft design during the World War II era, as shapes and capabilities were forced to advance in large increments. It took several years to match and then eclipse the German design geniuses.

By the end of the war and the late 1940s, momentum was clearly accelerating aviation technology at a near-quantum pace. Aircraft were advancing and eclipsing concurrent design studies by the day, not the decade. Given the notion that the United States had survived the war without destruction to any of its infrastructure, the country was leaping ahead in manufacturing and development of cutting-edge aircraft designs. In an ironic twist, the Cold War was now advancing the state of the art in aviation to favor the military airplanes rather than the civilian types. The dichotomy of the 1930s had reversed itself.

By 1954, the United States Air Force was flying large, heavy aircraft like the Boeing B-47 Stratojet at routine speeds of nearly 600 mph and altitudes exceeding 40,000 feet. Their range was spectacular as well, especially in the developing B-52 Stratofortress. The globe was rapidly beginning to shrink. However, the

Boeing's revolutionary B-47 Stratojet set the standard for Jet Age design when it first flew in 1947. Powered by six General Electric J47 turbojets and capable of being refueled in flight, the B-47 projected American aerial might during the early years of the Cold War. The big jet also gave Boeing a tremendous advantage in structural engineering and manufacturing prowess that would lead to the development of a new company-funded four-engine jet transport. (National Archives via Dennis R. Jenkins)

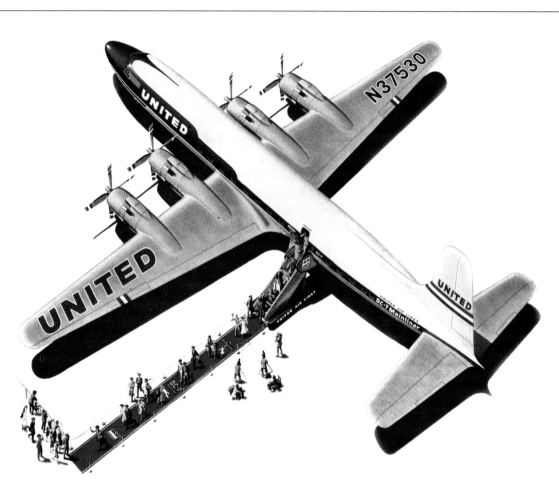

Enjoy "Red Carpet" service on United Air Lines' <u>new</u> DC-7s
...nation's fastest airliners, nonstop coast to coast!

You can look forward to "red carpet" service when you travel on one of United's de luxe DC-7s like "the Hollywood" or "the Continental." It's in keeping with the luxury you enjoy every mile of the way on the nation's newest, fastest and most comfortable airliners!

On United's DC-7s you relax in deep, richly upholstered seats ...you're served beverages, and delicious, full-course meals prepared by United's famous chefs...there are games, magazines, music... other service "extras" in the famous Mainliner® manner.

Cruising at 365 m.p.h. in the smooth upper air, you enjoy the added comfort of improved soundproofing, automatic pressurization, and air conditioning that keeps the cabin ever-fresh.

Also — your luggage gets "white glove treatment." It's stowed in a special compartment (exclusive with United) adjoining the main cabin for extra-fast delivery upon arrival.

For the finest service in air transportation, fly United's great Mainliner fleet. For reservations, call or write United or an Authorized Travel Agent.

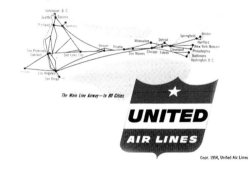

The Main Line Airway—to 80 Cities

UNITED
AIR LINES

Copr. 1954, United Air Lines

Representing the peak of modern American illustration were the famed, colorful airline ads of the 1950s. Painted by such commercial illustration legends as Joe Henninger and Ren Wicks, these glorious vistas often showed passengers boarding a sleek, giant, modern airliner with the ever-present red carpet and stanchions standing at the ready. Here we see the typical ad showing a bird's-eye view of a United DC-7 deplaning its happy passengers on an equally typical beautiful sunny day. Note the bevy of press photographers taking pictures of the Hollywood movie stars who were sure to be aboard. (Mike Machat Collection)

best speeds production commercial aircraft of the time could muster were in the 300-mph-plus range. This was a more-than-200-mph differential between military and civilian airplane types! (Of course, had the Republic Rainbow actually been consummated, speeds would have been half this.) And if one includes the fighter aircraft in the inventory or in flight test in 1954, the once-elusive speed of sound was being easily exceeded on a daily basis, and advanced experimental aircraft were now attaining more than *twice* that speed.

As tantalizing as these now-shattered limitations were, reality within the airline boardrooms dictated an attitude that was something entirely different. The prevailing thinking was that jet propulsion was too much of everything: too radical, too dangerous, too undependable, too fuel consumptive, and too expensive. "Best to leave all this risk taking to those jet jockeys in the military, and if you want to know why we think this way, just look across the pond at Britain's travails with their Comet," said the airline mavens. Flying in the stratosphere and utilizing kerosene blasting out of a pipe was just too dangerous for commercial applications. The airlines had just spent a decade and a half, and lots of advertising dollars, convincing people that airline flying was *safe* and *dependable*. No risks for us, thank you, said the airline bosses. Boeing, however, had other ideas.

What transpired when the prototype XB-47 was pulled out into the Seattle sunshine for the first time in late 1947 was nothing less than the standing of the aviation world on its proverbial head. This included the airline business as well, for every aspect of engineering that Boeing pioneered with its revolutionary Stratojet (which begat the even larger B-52) was transferred to its Model 367-80 prototype jet transport and the 707 jetliner. As a matter of fact, all basic high-Mach-number transports from the B-47 onward have been shaped to include the basic tenets developed in Seattle all those many years ago. That single airplane was absolutely transformational in nature.

In 1950, William Allen, Boeing's president, and his Chief Engineer for Preliminary Design, Maynard Pennell, visited the Farnborough Airshow in England to view the de Havilland Comet for the first time. After the fly-by in the afternoon, Allen asked Pennell what he thought of the English jetliner. "It's a very good airplane," Pennell responded. "Do you think we could build one as good?" asked Allen. "Better," said Pennell. "Much better." And they did.

From the point in May 1954 when the Dash 80 was rolled out at Renton, Washington, until the first jetliner revenue flight in late 1958, airline trepidation would slowly but inexorably start crumbling, bit by bit, just

President William Allen and the Boeing board of directors literally bet the company with a decision in 1952 to launch the 707 jet transport. Employees and the media gathered at the company's Renton, Washington, plant to witness the prototype Model 367-80 rollout on May 15, 1954. (Boeing/Jon Proctor Collection)

like a sand castle in the surf, until finally, outright enthusiasm was the order of the day in those staid boardrooms. But you can't run an airline operation without passengers. What did the folks at home think about all of this?

The postwar period, especially in the United States, was filled with one breakthrough or broken record after another. Pilots were already flying in jets or rocket-powered airplanes. Space travel was on everybody's mind, the Air Force and Navy leading the way in both instances. Cars that flew, houses that were smart enough to clean themselves and cook for us— everything futuristic was now within our grasp.

Of course we should be flying coast-to-coast in jet-liners! *Of course* we should link the continents by over-flying great bodies of water at high speeds and altitudes with the reliability and simplicity that the turbine engine promised. Even linking city centers via jet-powered heli-copters was just around the corner. It seemed everything we could imagine, we could do. The age of optimism had coupled with the age of speed, and air travelers couldn't wait to experience the jetliner. The airlines were begin-ning to lay the foundation to indulge these yearnings, and the world was ready to enjoy The Next Great Thing: the Jet Age.

In the meantime, however, passengers would have to be content with wide seats and lovely meals in airlin-ers, which were taking 9 or 10 hours to cross the coun-try, and with a stop or two at that. What a study in contrast between those futuristic articles we read in *LIFE*, *POST*, or *Collier's*, and the realities of commer-cial aviation at the time.

Aircraft of the Era

With four-engine land airplanes now firmly estab-lished as the ultimate means for long-distance interna-tional travel and U.S. domestic transportation as well, airliners had indeed become the "giant silver queens of the skies" as the marketing world liked to call them. The next logical step in their continuing evolution would be to equip them with uprated engines, more comfortable passenger cabins, and a steadily improving air travel infrastructure that made flying safer and more reliable.

Douglas DC-6B

As the competitive tussle continued between Douglas and Lockheed's four-engine products, the next round of "one-upsmanship" went to Santa Monica and its new and improved version of the DC-6.

Stretched by 60 inches (as was the all-cargo DC-6A), the DC-6B iteration of the basic design thus became the quintessential airline transport of the late prop era, and came to be known in retrospect as the

Considered by many to be the "thoroughbred" of piston-powered transports, the Douglas DC-6B was one of the best propliners ever built. This inflight photo of a Western Airlines DC-6B in flight highlights the airplane's clean and purposeful lines. An outgrowth of the regular DC-6, the -6B featured club seating and two more win-dows ahead of the wing, plus uprated engines and overall refinement throughout. (Douglas Aircraft Company/Mike Machat Collection)

United Air Lines Douglas DC-6B on the ramp with the final assembly hangar of Douglas Aircraft's Santa Monica plant visible in the background. All Douglas air-liners from the DC-1 to the DC-7 were built at this facil-ity, but manufacturing moved to the larger Long Beach airport with the advent of the first Douglas jetliners. Note cowl flaps for the aircraft's Pratt & Whitney R-2800 Double Wasp radials in the full open position on the engine nacelles. (Craig Kodera Collection)

"thoroughbred." This proclamation is based strictly on economical operations data, and not subjective criteria, for the -6B was the most cost-effective piston transport available. Its seat-mile numbers spoke for themselves, and combined with the ultrareliable Pratt & Whitney R-2800 engines, this airplane became the workhorse of the airlines.

As the orders arrived at Douglas, a key aspect to the customer base was noted: All the trunk airlines in the United States, including Pan American, bought the -6B for their fleets. (All except TWA, that is.) Those airlines new to the DC-6 series were current Constellation operators! The Douglas design really stole the show from Lockheed as far as economical and reliable air transportation was concerned. Western Air Lines was able to build its entire operation around the DC-6B, and in fact was the third-largest operator of the airplane, with 31 in its fleet. (Pan American flew the highest number; United Air Lines was second.)

American and United began DC-6B service in April 1951 and Pan American inaugurated Tourist Class service across the North Atlantic with its airplanes. As the final show of its popularity and prowess, it is interesting to note that the last DC-6B was delivered one month before the final Douglas propliner of any kind, a DC-7C. The -6B also remained in operational service in the United States through the end of the 1960s—well into the timeframe when the new jetliners ruled the skies. Overall, the DC-6B made quite a name for itself, selling a total of 288 airframes to the airlines.

Lockheed 1049 Super Constellation

Stretching the basic design of an airliner airframe first began in the 1930s with the DC-1 being lengthened into the DC-2. The Constellation was the perfect candidate for lengthening and weight increase due to the amount of power built into its Wright R-3350 engines. With the desire to accommodate either more range or more passengers (Tourist Class was becoming a reality for the airline companies), Lockheed added 18 feet 4¾ inches to the basic 749 fuselage and created the Model 1049 Super Constellation. An impressive total of 550 new design features were added to the airplane, including larger cockpit and cabin windows, larger vertical stabilizers, new fuel tankage, metal-covered ailerons, and a new electrical system.

The first "stretched" Constellation, Model 1049, featured an 18-foot 4¾-inch increase in its fuselage. TWA began painting its aircraft fuselages white to reflect heat and provide cooler cabin interiors, and to comply with a request from the Department of Defense that American transports be painted white to avoid looking like bare-metal Soviet bombers. (This was requested to avoid confusing USAF Air Defense Command interceptor pilots who were "scrambled" into the air to identify potential enemy bogies!) TWA used the Model 1049 to inaugurate the first transcontinental nonstop service in October 1953, and kept its 10-aircraft fleet on domestic flights. (TWA/Jon Proctor Collection)

Eastern bought 14 of these airplanes and TWA bought 10. The low number of total orders for this specific version indicates that the airplane was, in essence, a transitional aircraft, giving it new capabilities, but not being quite as advanced as later versions that would incorporate turbo-compound engines, or perhaps even turboprop powerplants such as the Allison T38 in a unique military configuration. What is significant, however, is that the Model 1049 confirmed that getting the most from a basic design by constantly improving it would pay huge dividends in the years immediately following this first stretch of the classic Constellation.

Convair 340

Jolted into reality by the large Martin orders, Convair began marketing the improved Model 240A, later renamed the 340, which not only leapfrogged the 404's attractiveness, but blunted a potential threat from Convair's East Coast rival.

One of the few major carriers to never operate the Douglas DC-3, National replaced its Lockheed Model 12 Lodestars with a dozen Convair 340s. (Ira Ward/Jon Proctor Collection)

In response to Martin's Model 404, Convair designers stretched the Convair 240 by 4 feet 6 inches, lengthened its wingspan, and nearly doubled fuel capacity to produce the Model 340; more than 200 civil versions were sold, including 26 to Braniff International Airways. Here, an example rests between flights at Kansas City Municipal Airport. (Bob Woodling)

The Model 340 stretched the 240 design by 4 feet 6 inches, increasing seating capacity to 44 passengers. Its wingspan was lengthened by 13 feet 11 inches, allowing nearly double the 240's fuel capacity, up to 1,900 gallons. Upgraded engines completed the package, which drew a 30-airplane order from United Air Lines, later growing to 55. The Model 340 "Cosmopolitan" enjoyed wide acceptance from the airline industry, both

United flew the largest fleet of Convair-Liners; 55 Model 340s served the carrier for more than 12 years without incurring a single passenger fatality. Mainliner Omaha awaits customers at its San Diego birthplace. (Jon Proctor)

in the United States and overseas. Supplementing the 209 civil versions built, the U.S. Navy and Air Force purchased an additional 102.

Boeing 377 Stratocruiser

Essentially a prewar design, Boeing's Model 377 was hatched from its military Model 367, designated the C-97 for cargo work, and KC-97 as an aerial tanker. It utilized the B-29 Superfortress wing and engines and answered Pan American Airways' performance requirement first circulated among aircraft builders in 1941. The carrier was looking to replace its flying boats with a landplane capable of carrying a 17,500-pound payload for 5,000 miles at 375 mph.

The result was one of the most luxurious airliners of the postwar era, with a cruising speed of 340 mph, a maximum payload of 25,000 pounds, an absolute range of 4,600 miles, with a ceiling altitude of more than 33,000 feet. Its Pratt & Whitney 28-cylinder, R-4360 Wasp Major engines were the most powerful ever built for commercial use but would ultimately prove to be troublesome, as were its propellers. Pan Am placed a $25 million launch order in December 1945 for 20 airplanes.

The "Strat" first flew on July 8, 1947, and entered airline service with Pan Am on April 1, 1949, between

The mighty Model 377 Stratocruiser, Boeing's first commercial airliner effort since the Model 307 Stratoliner, was brought about by mating the military B-50 Superfortress wings, engines, and tail planes to a twin-lobe fuselage. Though loved by passengers for its luxurious interior cabin, the Stratocruiser proved to be complicated to maintain and expensive to operate. In the end, only 56 civil versions were built. (Boeing/Jon Proctor Collection)

NEW YORK TO LOS ANGELES— NONSTOP AT LAST!

A wonderfully staged picture shows off TWA's new 1049 Super Constellation. With the airline serving Burbank, it was relatively easy to set up such photos at the same airport where the Connies were built. (TWA/Jon Proctor Collection)

Reliable coast-to-coast nonstop flights could, theoretically, have begun with the introduction of DC-4s and Constellations following the end of World War II. In fact, TWA operated one "scheduled" Los Angeles to New York nonstop on February 3, 1948, when a fierce winter storm covered the Midwest. Flight 12's regular Kansas City and Chicago stops were canceled and the Model 049 Connie covered the 2,470-mile flight in 6 hours 55 minutes.

While air travel began its rapid growth during this time period, the number of transcontinental tickets probably did not justify such flights. Although the market was sufficient by the early 1950s, and aircraft could stretch their legs across the country nonstop, they did not. Why?

In his book, *Howard Hughes and TWA*, Robert W. Rummel wrote that the airline's traffic managers argued against the longer flights, based on their belief that passengers wanted an en-route stop to get out and stretch their legs, and that no one wanted to fly nonstop across North America for up to nine hours. Perhaps a more important reason was that pilot contracts and U.S. federal air regulations prohibited flights of more than eight hours without an augmented crew, which would also result in additional costs to the airline. TWA operated its transatlantic flights this way as a matter of expediency, but not on long domestic routes where crew changes could be easily carried out.

When American Airlines announced plans to begin coast-to-coast nonstop service with its new DC-7s, TWA quickly inaugurated its own nonstop service and upstaged the competition. On October 19, 1953, "Ambassador" Flight 2, an overnight service from Los Angeles to New York-Idlewild, operated with the Model 1049 Super Constellation, which could barely cover the distance in less than eight hours; it was scheduled for 7 hours 55 minutes. Prevailing winds would not permit a westbound flight within the time constraint, so a 15-minute stop was made at Chicago for a crew change with no local traffic allowed!

Not to be upstaged, American Airlines quickly retaliated with DC-7 "Nonstop Mercury" flights in both directions, on November 29. Although the Douglas was faster than the Super Connie, and flew an eastbound 7-hour 15-minute schedule, it could not

reliably operate its under-eight-hour westbound time frame, a fact quickly pointed out by American's pilot union but quietly ignored by federal officials. More than a dozen modifications were carried out in an effort to squeeze extra speed from the DC-7's R-3350 engines, but this was not enough to resolve the dilemma.

Then, early in 1954, government restrictions were lifted to make transcontinental nonstops in excess of eight hours "legal," and American revised its westbound schedule to 8 hours 15 minutes. While TWA and its pilots reached agreement on overtime for duty in excess of eight hours and began nonstops in both directions, American and its crews deadlocked over the work rules. The entire pilot workforce walked out on July 31, 1954.

The company's legendary president, C. R. Smith, on military leave at the time, returned infuriated about the work stoppage. He quickly reached an agreement with the pilots that called for extra pay on flights—on DC-7s only—exceeding eight hours, ending a 24-day strike. TWA retained a bit of an advantage with eight sleeping berths available on its Super Connies, unlike the DC-7's standard "day plane" configurations, but both carriers offered lounges and lavish meal service. United Air Lines, which received its first DC-7s six months behind American Airlines, launched nonstops from San Francisco to New York—again eastbound only—on June 1, 1954; westbound flights began nearly a year later.

TWA's 1049 Super Constellations featured an aft seven-seat lounge. On longer flights the three seats located across the back of the cabin were covered to provide table space for a snack buffet, as seen in this cabin mockup photo.
(Byron Schmidt)

Douglas DC-7s dominate the American Airlines concourse at Los Angeles in this 1957 photo. A large Douglas Aircraft Company sign mounted atop the El Segundo facility that built Navy jets is visible in the background. This sign would later be moved to Douglas's new Long Beach plant when DC-8 production began, and is still there today, proudly preserved by the city of Long Beach. (Los Angeles World Airports)

San Francisco and Honolulu. Its furnishings included provisions for 28 upper- and lower-bunk berths. In a day configuration, the airplane could accommodate up to 103 passengers, and featured a unique 14-passenger lounge located below the main cabin. Only 56 Stratocruisers were built, for Pan Am (21, including the prototype), Northwest (10), American Overseas (8), BOAC (10), and United (7). Northwest was the last of the original customers to withdraw the type, on September 15, 1960.

Unlike surplus DC-3s and DC-4s, used Stratocruisers were difficult to place with second-tier operators. Knowing this, the type's original owners traded them in to aircraft manufacturers as down payments on jet equipment. Transocean Air Lines, then the largest non-scheduled airline, bought 14 Stratocruisers that Boeing acquired in this fashion. Barely two years later, the airline went bankrupt and its Strats were sold

at auction with only four in flyable condition. A few other short-lived attempts were made to utilize second-hand examples, but did not succeed.

The only long-term success realized with second-hand Stratocruisers came in the form of Aero Spacelines' radical modification to the airframe that resulted in the "Pregnant Guppy," with an enlarged fuselage capable of ferrying oversize cargo. On the military side, the Israeli Air Force picked up five ex-Pan Am 377s for use as freighters, two of which were converted to swing-tail configurations.

Although Boeing could not claim great success from its civil Stratocruiser version, it prospered from the construction of 888 C-97/KC-97 military variants. But Stratocruiser production was important in allowing the manufacturer to keep its hand in the civilian airliner market, which it would begin dominating in the 1960s, with its revolutionary turbojet 707 series.

Chapter Four

PROMISE OF
THINGS TO COME
(1954-1956)

Gold Cup Roll, *Tex Johnston's aerobatic Boeing 367-80 in August 1955.* (Mike Machat)

Boeing, primarily a builder of bombers and transports, designs a brand-new prototype that will change the heady game of airliner manufacturing forever. Developed to become a high-speed tanker for the Air Force's emerging fleet of new jet aircraft, this four-engine transport becomes an obvious candidate for airline service as well. The public begins to embrace the concept of air travel by jet, and the revolutionary Boeing 707 is born.

The 367-80: Boeing's $15 Million Gamble

This airplane's shape didn't just suggest the Jet Age, it *was* the Jet Age. With design features such as a rakish 35-degree swept wing and podded turbojets lifted directly from Boeing's new B-47 strategic bomber, the Model 367-80 prototype, or "Dash 80" as it came to be known in industry circles, epitomized jet travel, and left Britain's formerly cutting-edge de Havilland Comet in the dust. Cruising high in the stratosphere at almost transonic speed, the Dash 80 symbolized what com-

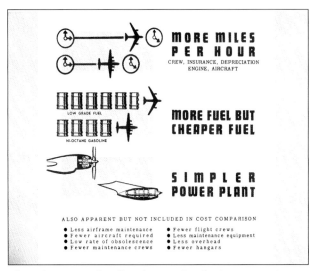

This chart graphically shows the fuel cost and time advantage of the Model 473 over existing propeller-driven airliners. Although this particular airplane was never produced, the writing was on the wall for a new generation of jet-powered transports to take the airline industry to its next level. (Craig Kodera Collection)

mercial jet travel would be like for the privileged passengers who would someday fly aboard a later production version of the airplane.

As with any radical new design, countless engineering studies resulting in numerous aircraft concepts are winnowed down to a smaller number of final configurations from which the actual prototype design is chosen. Emerging from this design process in October 1950 was the Boeing Model 473, an airliner featuring a double-lobed and truncated Stratocruiser-type fuselage. Swept and tapered vertical and horizontal stabilizers from the B-47 were mounted on the rear fuselage, while double-podded engines were slung from its swept wing at mid-span, one pod per side. Similar in size to the largest DC-7s and Constellations of the time, this distinctive new design looked arresting to the casual viewer but somehow appeared "not quite ready for prime time."

Conceived from the outset as more of a marketing study than an actual "hard" design concept, the 473 was to have a gross weight of 135,000 pounds and a cruising speed of 500 mph at 40,000 feet. This was unheard-of performance for its day, especially with Britain's Comet still two years away from entering passenger service. Cargo capacity of the 473 was to be 5,000 pounds distributed in two separate lower-fuselage baggage compartments, one fore and one aft of the wing. Powerplants were to be four unspecified turbojets in the 9,500-pound-thrust category, and with its military-type drag chute, the airplane was intended to be able to operate from existing runways at any major airport in the world.

By 1954, however, two major developments had a profound effect on the future of commercial air travel.

Artist's rendering of the Model 473 in flight shows the influence of Boeing's C-97/Stratocruiser with its similar-looking nose section and double-lobe fuselage. Engine pod design was lifted directly from the B-52 Stratofortress. (Craig Kodera Collection)

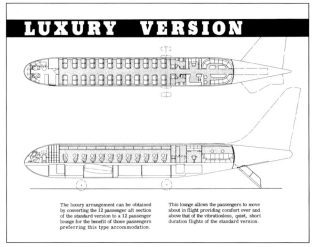

Model 473 Inboard Profile shows the passenger cabin arrangement to best advantage. Considering that airliners of this time period carried a payload of about 50 passengers, this concept must have seemed gigantic by comparison. (Craig Kodera Collection)

First, as previously noted, the de Havilland Comet entered service in May 1952, but was subsequently grounded within two years, after its infamous series of accidents. Second, Boeing froze the design for its new "prototype jet transport" into a sleeker configuration with four jet engines, each in their own separate underwing nacelle, a stubbier vertical fin, and a more airliner-like cockpit design. Disguised with a deceptive "Model 367" designation (used internally by the company for its KC-97 military tanker/transport version of the Stratocruiser), this larger, faster, and more powerful design was the eightieth configuration considered. Hence, the official name for Boeing's new jet prototype became the 367-80.

Constructed in a special walled-off and highly secure area of Boeing's historic Renton, Washington, facility, the "Dash 80" was built in only 18 months, and was rolled out for Boeing employees and industry representatives on May 15, 1954. This one-of-a-kind proof of concept demonstrator was unlike any other airplane ever seen at that time. Painted in a striking school-bus-yellow and chocolate-brown color scheme, the jet was 128 feet long with a 130-foot wingspan and a tail height of 38 feet. The engines were Pratt & Whitney's new J57 turbojets, and the airplane's main landing gear sported four wheels on each side instead of the traditional two. Anyone who saw the Dash 80 knew it was something special. What they didn't know was that this airplane would change air travel forever by siring an entire family of jet transports that would reduce travel times between any two places on earth by a staggering 50 percent.

Christened by Mrs. William Boeing as the "airplane of tomorrow," the 367-80 soon underwent preparation for its first flight. After a series of rigorous systems checks and taxi tests, the giant craft lifted off from Renton's runway for the first time on July 15, 1954,

The airplane that started it all, Boeing's futuristic 367-80 jet transport prototype. This airplane gave the world its first glimpse of future air travel when it took to the skies in July 1954, and provided a taste of things to come as it set one speed record after another traveling across the country on publicity and demonstration tours. (Harry Gann via Mike Machat Collection)

piloted by Boeing's Chief Test Pilot, A. M. "Tex" Johnston. The unique thing about that first flight is that there had been no airline orders placed for the airplane whatsoever. Not one! Then, as the new prototype began to demonstrate what a large jet-powered transport could do, the world began to take notice. So did the United States Air Force, which was in dire need of a faster aerial-refueling aircraft to service its new fleet of jet-powered strategic bombers and tactical fighters just then entering the inventory.

Boeing quickly "put its money where its mouth was" by flying the Dash 80 on a series of impressive demonstration flights, taking any number of special industry guests and aviation luminaries for their first rides in a jet-powered aircraft. Names like USAF Chief of Staff, General Curtis LeMay soon graced the passenger roster as he evaluated the airplane for its impending role as the Air Force's new "flying gas station," to be known as the KC-135 Stratotanker. Excitement was building around the new jet, as the public's anticipation of flying in America's first jet airliner grew in magnitude. The Dash 80 was catapulted to national attention when Tex Johnston performed not one, but two barrel rolls while flying over the famed Gold Cup speed-boat races at Seattle's Sea Fair in August 1955. Asked later by Bill Boeing why he did it, Johnston replied in his typical droll manner, "I was selling airplanes."

On one memorable demonstration flight, Johnston was told by the Boeing Field tower to remain in position on the ramp with engines running. It was a typical rainy spring day in Seattle, and Tex noticed a company car racing out to the airplane. Emerging from the back seat was a tall, slim figure clutching his raincoat tightly to his body. Rushing up the boarding stairs, the gentleman walked into the cockpit and unceremoniously took his place in the airplane's jump seat. Tex turned around to greet him, and shook hands with none other than Charles A. Lindbergh, acting in an advisory capacity for Pan American World Airways. According to Johnston, Lindbergh later sat in the co-pilot's seat and even took the controls of the Dash 80 while flying over Portland, Oregon, at 600 mph. Johnston marveled at how much aviation progress had been made in the less-than-thirty-year time span since Lindbergh's epic solo transatlantic flight in 1927!

On October 16, 1955, with William Boeing and other VIP guests on board, Johnston flew the Dash 80 from Boeing Field in Seattle to Washington D.C., reaching a top speed of 620 mph and arriving at Andrews Air Force Base in only 3 hours 48 minutes. The fact that this flight established a new U.S. coast-to-coast cross-country record did not go unnoticed by the world's airlines, and orders for a slightly larger production version of the new jet, called the 707, started coming in to Boeing in impressive numbers.

Boeing's first airline order was from Pan American when its President, Juan Trippe, ordered 20 of the new jets. American's C. R. Smith ordered 30, and then came Continental and Braniff orders. Surprisingly, the first foreign air carrier to order the 707 was Belgium's Sabena, followed by Air France. Bringing up the rear in this initial batch was TWA with its pivotal order for 8 of the new jetliners, bringing the total 707 order book to 81 airplanes. Although this will be covered in more detail later, it should be mentioned that by this time, rival manufacturer Douglas Aircraft, still king of the airliner builders, had recorded 124 orders for its similar-looking, but yet-to-be-flown DC-8 Jetliner.

For awhile, it appeared that Boeing would never be able to break the decades-old stigma of being in Douglas's shadow as an airliner builder, but when BOAC, Lufthansa, El Al, and Air India lined up to order longer-range versions of the 707, Boeing's tally grew to 145 before the DC-8 ever flew, and the race was on. As we will see later, both of these jetliners evolved into larger and more improved airplanes, but once Boeing gained the advantage and pulled ahead of Douglas, there was no turning back. With its Dash 80, Boeing literally "bet the company" that this revolutionary new aircraft would eventually become a commercial success, and it will be considered for all of history to be one gutsy $15 million gamble that paid off quite handsomely.

Manufacturer's Dilemma: Turboprop vs. Turbojet

Despite the success of Boeing's prototype jet transport, not everyone in the airline industry was convinced that turbojets were the ultimate answer to airliner development.... Jet engines explode! Jet engines use too much fuel, and they might even catch surrounding airport structures on fire. They are unreliable and uneconomical, and will cause a fortune to be spent on lengthening runways and expanding terminal facilities. The answer is no, we're not going to fly airliners powered by jet engines!

So went the thinking in the U.S. airline industry immediately after World War II. And why not? The Jumo and BMW axial-flow turbine engines that came out of Germany after the occupation had been years ahead of their time as far as known metallurgy and materials were concerned. These engines lasted, if the fighter squadron was even lucky enough, perhaps 100 flying hours at best before they totally disintegrated.

In England and via license in the United States, centrifugal-flow jet engines seemed to be the answer to those reservations, with the possible exception of catching on fire. Their ruggedness and simplicity made them more viable powerplants, and the military was anxious, if not simultaneously full of trepidation, at the thought of putting them into routine operational use.

As mentioned previously, the notion of using new turbojet engines for commercial airline applications were pipe dreams more than reality prior to 1950, although the wonderful Avro Jetliner would probably have changed all that (see Chapter 1 sidebar "Avro Jetliner: The Other First Jet," page 17). The de Havilland Comet 1 almost did by 1952. And in 1954, at the introduction of the Dash 80 from Boeing, the tide was finally starting a slow turn in favor of pure jet airliners.

By the late-1940s, however, it was becoming apparent to airplane industry observers that postwar England had warmly embraced jet power, in all its forms. Eventually, from 1948 to 1958 no fewer than 10 different airliner designs came off the drawing boards either incorporating or anticipating the use of *turbo-prop* engines. Existing airplanes were also modified with turbine-propeller engines either experimentally or as operational upgrades. Why did they utilize turbo-prop technology to this extent? England was the leader in pure-jet technology, so why were they dithering with propellers (or airscrews, as they were called in that country)?

Well, the answers to these questions are many. Foremost was that jet engines at the time were just too underpowered to carry enough weight, and hence provide enough payload and range for an airliner. Being underpowered also meant using long runways. (Most piston propliners of the era required as little as 2,500 feet of runway for takeoff while jets would easily require twice that.) Jet engines also took an appreciable amount of time to come up to full-power RPM from flight idle settings (known as "spool-up" time for the axial-flow designs). Pilots had to really anticipate the need for power far in advance. Unlike the piston engine, there was no instantaneous surge of thrust from the jets when one moved the throttle forward, which is never a safe situation in an airplane.

Enter the turbine-propeller combination. In a turboprop package, the jet engine is linked to a propeller via a reduction gearbox. The jet engine is typically spinning at a constant 100-percent rpm, while throttle controls are actually changing only the pitch of the blades, therefore allowing for the all important instantaneous thrust applications by the pilot. The added thrust of turbine efflux combined with the strong and immediate pull of the propeller makes up for the lack of thrust coming from an early pure-jet engine alone. Additionally, the air being moved over the wings from the propeller also adds an appreciable amount of self-generated lift. These obvious advantages were not lost on engineers and airline bosses alike, and it became a natural course of action for the world's airlines, and hence their suppliers, to seriously consider turboprop powerplants.

Decisions, Decisions

In Britain, turboprops already ruled the airways, from the small Miles Marathon to the gigantic Saunders-Roe Princess flying boat. Short or long range, these new hybrid engines flew on them all. In America, many major aircraft manufacturers were contemplating and developing their own turbine-propeller-powered airframes. There was the giant XC-132 cargo carrier from Douglas, and even Boeing's first B-52 strategic bomber design concept was a turboprop! All existing airplanes were being designed around future turboprop powerplants (as noted in the sections on Lockheed's Constellation series). But these same companies were also concurrently thinking pure jet, which brings us to the DC-7D.

As early as 1952, Douglas had secretly established a jet-engine airliner study group. For public consumption, however, and that of the airline chiefs, Douglas later offered rather half-heartedly what everyone considered a stopgap airplane powered by RB.109 turboprop engines from Rolls-Royce. The aircraft was based on the DC-7C airframe, but had a swept vertical stabilizer and a 40-inch fuselage stretch. C. R. Smith at American was interested, but at the urging of Art Raymond, Vice President of Engineering at Douglas, Donald Douglas made the decision to skip the turboprop and go directly to pure jet power. The result of that pivotal decision was the DC-8.

Facing all the other airliner manufacturers at that time was the very same choice Don Douglas had to

Remember the Republic RC-2 Rainbow shown on page 11 in Chapter One? This design concept was resurrected in the mid-1950s as a veritable "last gasp" from the company to attempt to harness the commercial airliner market. Looking like a cross between various aircraft designs from Vickers, Fokker, and Potez, the Turboprop Rainbow never left the drawing boards at Farmingdale. (Cradle of Aviation Museum Archives via Mike Machat Collection)

make. Should they play the game by putting off the inevitable transition to pure jets and produce a turbo-prop airliner? If they did, they had to realize that the market was going to be medium to small at best. There was, therefore, every reason to believe that supplying such an airplane would be a money-losing proposition. And yet, if the manufacturers jumped right to jets with all their inherent risks, would the airlines be willing to jump with them?

In the meantime, minds were made up at American and Eastern Air Lines to ask for bids on a clean-sheet-of-paper turboprop design, with Lockheed's Electra emerging as the winner of that competition. This suited Lockheed who had lost a "promised" contract for the Air Force's new four-engine jet tanker, which steered them directly to the consolation prize of turboprop power. By mid-1955, American had signed on for 35 Electras while Eastern ordered 40.

While Boeing had flown its Dash 80 prototype and Douglas was planning its own new DC-8 Jetliner, airlines that wanted to hedge their jet bets bought Electras as well to "complement" their pending pure-jet fleet. Marketing logic dictated that the intermediate technology of the turbine-propeller would be just fine for flying from New York to Chicago, or even all the way from New York to Los Angeles, just in case the jets didn't quite work out. As an aside, Western Airlines with its new route authority to Hawaii a few years later was quite willing to use Electras rather than buy or lease the 707. For Western, the Electra was the wonder

On the West Coast another stillborn concept was envisioned but then abandoned when Douglas decided to forge ahead with a pure-jet airliner called the DC-8. By not building the interim Douglas DC-7D Turboprop shown in this concept rendering, Douglas left the task of building America's only turboprop-powered airliner to Lockheed with its Electra design. (Craig Kodera Collection)

airplane of the era; such was its economy of operation, flexibility, and quasi-jet-like speed. Western did not order pure jets until 1960.

Once all was said and done in the saga of the turboprop in America, things turned out pretty much as expected. The British supplied the first round of airplanes: Viscounts to Capital and Northeast, where Britannias were also nearly a reality for both carriers. The Electra was built for the second round of equipment upgrades, delivering a larger airplane with greater range. With only 170 aircraft produced, however, the Electra program ultimately lost money, as predicted. At the smaller-size end of the spectrum, Fairchild license-built the twin-engine F-27 turboprop from Fokker for local service airlines, with a total of 129 coming from its Hagerstown, Maryland, plant.

By 1959, the surprising quality, reliability, and ready acceptance by passengers of the pure jets, combined with a sudden reality that more airline seats were needed in the market, accelerated the arrival of shorter-range jetliners such as the Caravelle, 720, 727, and finally, the DC-9 in the mid-1960s. This negated the need for further large turboprop designs, and early-on stifled sales of the Electra (and in Britain, the Vanguard). The F-27 soon became a victim of its own success in stimulating new traffic at the small airlines, for it rapidly became too small, and larger equipment was ordered rather than more of the basic F-27.

Truly niche aircraft, the turboprops of the 1950s provided a valuable transition, or "bridge," in the progression from props to jets. But the window of opportunity was quite small, and for one manufacturer, Lockheed, the decision to spurn pure jets would have competitive ramifications for years to come, completely changing the dynamics of the market and its players in the new world order of commercial jet airliners.

Aircraft of the Era

By the year 1953, the farsighted growth-capable designs of both the Douglas and Lockheed Aircraft Companies began to pay off handsomely for the airline industry. Proper engines mated to stretched and refined airframes created whole new levels of opportunity for airline operators and passengers alike.

Lockheed 1049C

As mentioned earlier, the Constellation was constantly being stretched and/or its gross weight was being continually increased beginning with the first Model 49. Now Lockheed mated the Wright R-3350 Turbo Compound engine to its recently lengthened 1049 airplane, and the correct balance of performance and capability aligned beautifully to produce a superior aircraft. Not quite the pinnacle of Constellation

Left: Nicely illustrating the concept of Eastern Air Lines' Chairman Eddie Rickenbacker's "Great Silver Fleet," this Lockheed Super C Constellation cruises through the Florida skies. (Eastern/Jon Proctor Collection)

Below: Rare photo from a historical perspective shows a 1049H, not a C; the giveaway is the window arrangement ahead of the props. This airplane was "delivered" to Seaboard & Western on February 13, 1957, and leased the same day to Eastern; one of five airplanes so leased for short-term work during the winter season. All were returned to Seaboard that following June. (Craig Kodera Collection)

Looking exactly like one of Eastern's new Super G Connies that had just entered the fleet, this interesting photo shows a 1049C passenger transport that has been converted to an all-freighter configuration. Note the Eastern DC-6B, DC-7B Golden Falcon, and Martin 404 parked in the background. (Eastern/Jon Proctor Collection)

Although this National DC-7 is a "B" model, it is externally identical to the standard DC-7. A further evolution of the DC-6B, the DC-7 established Douglas as a builder of transcontinental commercial transports. The improved DC-7B and intercontinental DC-7C would complete the series. (Mike Machat Collection)

development, the "Super C" model was nevertheless a huge step forward for Connie operators.

KLM was the first airline to operate the airplane starting in August 1953 with nonstop flights from New York to Amsterdam. Again, these were eastbound non-stops only, but that was still a great step forward, with Air France soon joining the trend with a nonstop from New York to Paris.

As part of the upgrade to the travel experience on the new larger aircraft, Lockheed commissioned Henry Dreyfuss to design unique interiors for passenger comfort and interest. He gave the Constellation wood paneling, defused lighting, classic fabrics in rearranged lounges, and colorful murals and maps on the walls. These features were the hallmark of Constellation flying. Passenger accommodation varied from 54 to 60 people in the "Intercontinental" layout (or just 47 folks in the "Siesta" floor plan), all the way up to 106 passengers in the "Inter-Urban" configuration. Overwater long-distance flying was still considered a luxury endeavor.

As with all the new Constellations, the airplane's structure was designed to allow for a 150,000-pound all-up weight should the day come when the series made the transition to turbine-propeller, or turboprop power. Now that would really be the ultimate!

Douglas DC-7

After what must have seemed like badgering by American's indomitable C. R. Smith, Douglas finally relented after reviewing operating cost benefits, and designed and built the DC-7. Adding another 40 inches to the DC-6B fuselage, the DC-7 really was not a completely new airplane. Much of the aircraft's structure and internal systems closely matched the DC-6B, which had tremendous advantages in terms of crew familiarity and training. However, with the addition of the R-3350 Turbo Compound engines, the airplane had 20-percent more power available than the R-2800-equipped DC-6B, and yet fuel consumption remained the same. More passengers per flight now meant that all these new features gave the airlines a nice, theoretical improvement in their bottom line.

The DC-7s entered revenue service on November 12, 1953. This latest Douglas airliner was also a fast airplane, eclipsing the Connie's cruise speed by some 30-plus mph. Its faster speed was critical in making the FAA flight-time requirement of less than eight scheduled hours for the flight crew, and after only a few short weeks of being the transcon champ, TWA's dominance fell to American Airlines.

From a "what's new" standpoint, the DC-7 series introduced the use of titanium in commercial airliners.

Cockpit of the DC-7 shows a well-laid-out instrument panel and control pedestal with the throttles, radio consoles, and trim wheel readily at hand. Flight Engineer's seat is facing forward in this photo giving him access to the control pedestal and the overhead panel controlling the aircraft's many onboard systems. Radio rack at left provided easy access for avionics maintenance personnel who may have had to change an entire radio unit or repair one of the many vacuum tubes contained therein. (Mike Machat Collection)

The landing gear doors were milled from this exotic and lightweight metal, thus reducing their weight by some 44 percent. Also novel on the aircraft was the engine-cooling ducting, which operated alternately during icing conditions. One other innovative feature of this fast airplane was the ability to place only its main landing gear in a down-and-locked position during rapid descents, thereby acting as speed brakes. We can only wonder how many false reports of "failed nose gear extension" observant pilots of other aircraft called in to the tower!

As we look back on the 1953 to 1954 period it seems as if Douglas had finally wrestled the fleeting lead from Lockheed in providing the next level of air service to the airlines and the public. However, as we all know, competition in the airline and airframe business can oftentimes be quite cutthroat, and can change dramatically at a moment's notice.

Convair 440

Minor modifications to Convair's Model 340 design brought about the Model 440 "Metropolitan," offering a slightly higher gross weight, reduced interior noise levels, and optional weather radar. Its exterior measurements were identical to the 340, and Continental Airlines introduced the type on March 8, 1956. Convair sold 100 modification kits to Model 340 operators in order to bring the earlier models up to near-440 standards.

With 199 civil and military 440 sales, Convair-Liner production ended in early 1958 after 1,076 units were manufactured, including the prototype Model 110. Among the last built were several airplanes that did not find buyers until 1960. Adapting turboprop engines to the type's airframe created the 500 and 600 series, stretching the aircraft's useful life by many years. Some are still flying today, more than 50 years later, a hearty tribute to a sturdy, well-built airframe.

The typical DC-7 main cabin provided passengers with all the comforts of home: curtained windows, wood paneling, plush seats, fresh fruit, and even pillows and blankets for taking an inflight nap. Note the Club Lounge at the extreme rear of the cabin, and the natty attire of the traveling public in the heyday of the propliner era. (Craig Kodera Collection)

The last and most successful Convair-Liner variant, its Model 440 Metropolitan reached civil and military sales of 199 airplanes. In addition 100 Model 340s were upgraded to 440 standards. A brand-new Metropolitan appears adjacent to the Convair plant at San Diego, apparently ready for a flight to Atlanta. (Convair/Jon Proctor Collection)

MAJOR U.S. AIRPORTS IN THE 1950s

Not a pasted-up or retouched image, this photo shows a well-staged scene with a Sabena Belgian Airlines DC-6 making a low high-speed pass over the main terminal building at New York's Idlewild Airport in the early 1950s. Carey bus at right provided convenient commuter service to the East Side Airline Terminal in Manhattan only 18 miles away. (Enell photo/Mike Machat Collection)

Despite Britain's false start with the Comet 1, and Boeing's new 367-80 jet transport being only a "proof-of-concept" prototype at this point, the promise of jet-powered commercial flight was becoming closer to reality with each passing week. As modern and accommodating as major U.S. airports may have been at that time, the need for expansion, improvement, and modernization for the new breed of jets was becoming increasingly apparent, as their unique operating requirements came into focus. First and foremost on this list were longer runways, requiring either expansion of existing facilities, or construction of a brand-new and much-larger airport farther away from the city center. This latter option, although more costly, allowed designers the distinct advantage of starting from scratch with whatever new design best suited local needs.

By taking a virtual tour of U.S. airports of this time period, we can see that the Northeast segment of the country provided the necessary passenger and cargo gateways to Europe and points east. For domestic travel, these same cities were the origins for trips westward all across the country to California and even Hawaii. Moving in a clockwise direction, we begin our tour with Logan International Airport in Boston, Massachusetts (BOS). Located on the tidal flats east of downtown Boston, this airport and its neighbor to the south, Idlewild Airport in New York (IDL), had nowhere to expand but outward on land-fill built into adjacent bays. New terminal complexes and vast ramp areas would be added to both these great airports within a decade.

Moving down the East Coast we come to National Airport in Washington, D.C. (DCA). Having opened in 1941, the airport had nowhere to expand geographically for the new jets. However, this scenario presented a brand-new opportunity for air-port planners in the Washington and Virginia metro-plex to consider—the design and construction of a brand-new mega-airport intended specifically for the Jet Age. Occupying more than 10,000 acres of virgin woodland located 45 minutes west of downtown

Washington, the new and futuristic Dulles International (DIA, later IAD) opened in 1962 with an average of only one or two aircraft movements per hour, a scenario that has changed dramatically since those early days.

Flying southward, we come to Atlanta, Georgia, where the local airport began life as Chandler Field. This airport remained quite adequate to accommodate the first generation of new jets, but then grew into the grand multi-terminal Hartsfield International (ATL) in the 1970s. Down in sunny southern Florida, Miami International (MIA) provided America's gateway to South America and the Caribbean, having done so since the 1920s. By 1959, the facility had expanded to absorb a neighboring Army airfield to the northwest, and soon became one of the largest jetports in the southern United States.

As we move toward the upper Midwest, we come across yet another example of a small, local, and convenient city airport that opened in 1927, but then had no physical room for expansion for the new jets. This airport would eventually give way to a new megajetport that would have to be built from scratch. Originally named Chicago Municipal Airport, Midway Airport (MDW) served as Chicago's home airport for decades, but was overshadowed by O'Hare International Airport (ORD). Originally built during World War II and opened for commercial traffic in 1955, O'Hare's new, larger, and vastly more modern terminal complex opened in 1962.

Following the Mississippi River southward, we come to a host of other mid-size city airports that began as waypoints for fuel and rest stops on transcontinental mail and passenger flights. These were Lambert Field in St. Louis, Missouri (STL), Kansas City in Kansas (KSC), and Love Field in Dallas, TX (DAL). These airports were eventually either augmented or replaced by larger complexes built on open land to the west.

Flying westward, perhaps one would stop at the Rocky Mountain home of Stapleton Field in Denver, Colorado (DEN), or Sky Harbor in Phoenix, Arizona (PHX), airports that both had room to grow for the big jets. Arriving on the West Coast we find Los Angeles International (LAX) and San Francisco International (SFO) in California, and Seattle/Tacoma's SeaTac in Seattle, Washington (SEA). All three of these airports expanded outward from their more modest 1950s configurations as the new jets entered service, with LAX moving to adjacent land immediately to the west, SFO expanding out into San Francisco Bay, and SeaTac growing on available open land to the north.

In all, America's major airports represented a host of problems and solutions for the geographic, logistical, and operational challenges posed by the worlds' first generation of modern jetliners. In the chapters that follow, we will see in more detail how new Jet Age terminals and airport layouts accommodated the needs of a new breed of air traveler and aircraft alike.

A typical busy morning scene at LAX reflects the pre-jet era of open concourses and loading steps. Taken in 1958, this photo reflects the epitome of the Golden Age of Air Travel. This exact location now serves as a maintenance and cargo area for a number of airlines serving LAX today, with the main airport having been extended to the west when the new jets arrived. (Los Angeles World Airports)

Chapter Five

COAST-TO-COAST IN ONLY EIGHT HOURS
(1953-1956)

Evening Star, a TWA Lockheed 1049G Constellation in 1956. (Mike Machat)

The American public is now awash in an exciting new world of science fiction, military jets, experimental rocket planes, and the coming space age. Aircraft manufacturers and airport planners alike are bracing for a new paradigm in air travel—the 100-passenger jetliner. Passenger travel by air is now being accepted as the norm and not the exception, and expec-tations run high for a day-and-age of jet-powered airliners.

Air Routes of the Time

Traveling across the United States between major cities was relatively simple in the early 1950s. Trunk carriers American, Northwest, United, and TWA offered direct, one-plane service to and from major destinations between the East and West Coast as long as one stayed within the central and northern states. Up and down the West Coast, travelers could choose between United and Western, while East Coast passengers, for the most part, relied on Eastern Airlines between New England and Florida. Delta operated a smaller route map, chiefly in the south, and Northeast Airlines, for the most part, served New England destinations.

Smaller cities and towns were the domain of 13 local service, or "feeder" carriers, that served a dual purpose. This second-level airline classification was established in 1944 on an experimental basis. Government-subsidized flights linked towns with populations as small as 5,000 inhabitants to major connecting cities. Permanent certification was finally granted to the 13 surviving operators (down from 20) in 1955. By the end of 1955, local service airline traffic had grown from 25,000 passengers in 1946 to nearly 3 million.

Local service carriers gradually added nearly 200 new destinations, a number that increased to 380 by 1957. Many were low-traffic stations taken over from trunk carriers that wanted to shed shorter routes. With these handovers, the local-service airlines continued to expand fleets, usually with DC-3s acquired from the same trunk carriers that surrendered the newly acquired towns and routes.

A large percentage of travelers utilized two airlines, and sometimes three, to reach their destinations. Trunk airlines formed "joint" fares with the locals and offered luggage checked through to the final destination, although passengers were obliged to check in again when changing carriers. Unlike today, the local carriers retained unique identities. United Express, Delta Connection, and similar monikers were unheard of in the 1950s.

Even some routes between major cities required the use of more than one airline, a constraint ignored by the Civil Aeronautics Board (CAB), which had sole authority to award new routes. Until the Southern

This local-service carrier began upgrading its DC-3 fleet with second-hand Convair 240s in mid-1955, offering its customers pressurized-cabin comfort and increased speed over the prewar fleet. (Jon Proctor Collection)

From Props to Jets

Transcontinental Route case granted broad single-carrier rights in 1961, air travel between Los Angeles and Florida required two or three carriers to complete the trip.

Some relief was offered on this and similar routes, in the form of "interchange" flights, where two or three airlines jointly operated single-plane, multi-stop service over a route. At intermediate points, one airline's flight crew would turn the aircraft over to another. On the Los Angeles to Miami run, for example, American operated as far as Dallas, where Delta crews took over for the segment to New Orleans, only to be relieved by National pilots and stewardesses, who took their passengers on to Florida. Separate ticket coupons were required for each carrier, but were taken by the originating carrier's boarding agent, thus giving the illusion of a single-carrier flight, although passengers were often startled to see a National Airlines DC-7 at Los Angeles, or an American Airlines Flagship at Miami.

Aircraft of the Era

At this point in the development of the competing Lockheed and Douglas designs, we arrive at the true pinnacle of development for each airplane in its *domestic* role. The maturity of the basic design now starts allowing the airlines real operational capability and flexibility, and we see the long-held promise of the ultimate four-engine-airliner concept becoming fulfilled by 1955.

Douglas DC-7B

A revised wing flap and an extra 12,000 pounds of gross weight differentiated the second member of the DC-7 family from the baseline airplane. The -7B appealed to domestic as well as a handful of international carriers, and served as an intermediate solution to the long-range requirements later satisfied by the DC-7C. (This novel approach of incorporating evolutionary design improvements to an existing airliner's airframe and powerplant would be to Douglas' advantage in the market a decade later with the expansion and improvement of its DC-8 Jetliner series.)

Pan American launched service with the new airplane on June 13, 1955, over its route from New York to London. These flights were performed nonstop with ease with Pan Am's configuration employing optional "saddle" auxiliary fuel tanks located on the aft upper engine nacelles, a feature that would become standard on the DC-7C. As mentioned earlier, the DC-7 was a fast airplane, and the "B" model was perhaps the fastest on record, having been clocked at sea level flying 410 mph over a closed speed course. This was 40 mph greater than the Super-G Constellation's published maximum speed at 20,000 feet. Every ounce of speed made a difference to the folks in the market-ing department, and contemporary advertising certainly reflected the "fastest service" angle for these airlines.

As with the DC-6B, several airlines that simultaneously operated Constellations also owned the DC-7B. National, Eastern, and South African come to mind, but Eastern's was the pivotal order for the airplane, 50 in total. The DC-7B was a special airplane for the usually spartan Eastern, and it was treated as such by its Chairman Eddie Rickenbacker. Upon introduction, the class of service and moniker for the airplane was Golden Falcon, and indeed the formerly red falcon in the roundel at the nose of the aircraft became a gold-leaf appliqué on the DC-7B. Passengers received a special blue-and-gold certificate printed on parchment paper signed by Rickenbacker himself, acknowledging his appreciation for their flying on his newest airplane.

The Golden Falcon's ultra-modern and visually striking cabin interior was designed by Harley Earl, General Motors' legendary chief designer and stylist. Fabrics were gold lamé for the curtains, blue-and-gold for the seat upholstery, and gold Mylar on fixtures throughout, with rich-looking dark-wood paneling completing the motif. Even the passenger air-conditioning outlets were painted gold. The first 30 aircraft delivered seated only 64 people in this opulent configuration, while the remaining 20 airplanes came from the factory in a more densely packed 93-seat Falcon Super Coach configuration.

A total of 112 DC-7B models were produced at Douglas' Santa Monica, California, plant.

Lockheed 1049 Super G Constellation

Meanwhile, over in Burbank, the folks at Lockheed were crafting their own "perfect" airliner of the times, known as the 1049 G Super Constellation, or simply, Super-G.

When one thinks of the Connie, one of the strongest details associated with any airplane comes to mind remembering the G model's optional and removable wingtip tanks. Lockheed certainly had a penchant for these types of auxiliary fuel tanks, and the Super-G was the best application of this technology ever used on a passenger airplane. Combined with a radar nose and the stretched fuselage of the earlier 1049, the Super-G package was by far the quintessential Constellation in terms of both style and practical design.

The G model's gross weight climbed to 137,500 pounds, which included 609 gallons of fuel housed in each of the wing tanks. Range, even at this weight, was a few hundred miles more than the DC-7B, giving the Connie a small leg up on its Douglas competition. The amount of fuel carried in the G airplane was an amazing two-thirds again as much as the original Model 49 from just 10 years prior. This is the type of refinement of

Not to be confused with today's Southwest Airlines, Southwest Airways was later renamed Pacific Air Lines and served local towns on the West Coast until it merged into Air West in 1968. It began operations in 1946. One of Southwest's original DC-3s is seen taxiing at Santa Maria, California. (William T. Larkins)

Two local-service carriers are represented in this picture taken at Kansas City in June 1962. Frontier would later acquire Central in a merger. Both airplanes are converted C-47 transports with original cargo door installations. (Bob Woodling)

Toward the end of its working life, an American Airlines DC-7B arrives at Phoenix Sky Harbor Airport, shortly before sunset on December 29, 1960. Boeing 707s and 720s were already quickly replacing Douglas propliners across America's system. (Jon Proctor)

Certificate provided to Eastern passengers during the DC-7B's first year of service stated, "In appreciation and recognition of your flight on Eastern Air Lines' new DC-7B luxury airliner, the 'Golden Falcon.'" (Mike Machat Collection)

design and growth-of-concept that we have referred to, and the manufacturers had really hit their strides with both the 1049G and DC-7B.

A total of 102 1049Gs were produced, with more than half being delivered to overseas carriers such as

This July 1956 photo shows the passenger's-eye view while boarding a brand-new Eastern Air Lines DC-7B Golden Falcon preparing to depart from Miami International Airport for New York's Idlewild Airport. (Sykes Machat photo)

KLM and Air France. In January 1955, Northwest Orient Airlines began transpacific service using G models to fly to Tokyo from Seattle via Honolulu and later, to Anchorage over the great circle route. On the other side of the globe, Lufthansa was having marvelous success with "The Senator Service" with its twice-weekly flights to the United States. Lufthansa configured its Super-Gs in a deluxe 32-seat cabin layout and this service was later extended to the airline's South American routes. For air passengers, this was undoubtedly the best time in the world to be flying aboard a new luxury airliner from Douglas or Lockheed.

SE 210 Caravelle I, IA, and III

There can only be one "first" of anything, and for rear-engined jet airliners, the Sud-Est SE 210 Caravelle proudly holds that honor. French aircraft manufacturers were identified by region, Nord (North), Sud-Ouest (Southwest), or Sud-Est (Southeast). Named for the small, swift, twin-masted sixteenth-century sailing ships that also became the aircraft's official logo, the Caravelle turned heads at the Paris Airshow when revealed to the public for the first time in 1957. However, the airplane's genesis dates back to the late-1940s when

Although Continental Airlines did not serve San Diego at the time, one of its DC-7Bs was photographed while operating a three-stop interchange service with American Airlines between Los Angeles and Houston in August 1959. (Jon Proctor)

Although an early Constellation operator, Eastern Air Lines turned to Douglas for a 50-strong fleet of DC-7Bs, which wore several variations of the company's colors. Two stewardesses are seen departing at the end of their duty day in December 1963 at New York's Idlewild Airport. Also known as New York International, the airport was officially renamed for slain President John F. Kennedy on Christmas Eve day that year. (Harry Sievers)

The Connie's classic lines are handsomely accentuated by wingtip fuel tanks in this overhead view taken at Kansas City. It was TWA's first airliner to feature two classes of service, with separate entry doors for each cabin section. (TWA/Jon Proctor Collection)

the French aircraft industry led the country back from the ruins of World War II by formulating a plan for the design and development of a new commercial airliner to be exported worldwide.

This airplane was to be a medium-size, medium-range jet transport intended to fill the apparent gap in new commercial aircraft sized just below larger, longer-range four-engine jetliner designs then on the drawing boards in England, Canada, and the United States. Initially called the X-200 and masterminded by Sud's brilliant Chief Engineer Pierre Satre, numerous configurations were proposed with the tenth design, or X-210, emerging as the most likely candidate for development. This was a three-engine aircraft called the Tri-Atar, which bore a striking resemblance to another airplane that would later be known as the Boeing 727. By 1951, capitalizing on improvements in jet powerplant technology, a twin-engine version of the X-210 came into focus, and the Caravelle was born.

Sporting twin Rolls-Royce Avon turbojets housed in slim nacelles mounted on the aircraft's aft fuselage, this new jetliner looked sleek, efficient, and practical, yet stylishly modern at the same time. With the engines at the rear, the Caravelle's slightly swept wings were left strictly to provide lift at maximum efficiency, giving the aircraft an impressive glide ratio of 19:1—the same as high-performance gliders of the time. The airplane's landing gear was also suitably short, giving it a low

stance, and allowing full maintenance and ramp service with only a few work stands required.

Passengers enjoyed another major benefit of the rear-mounted engines: The painful roar of exhaust noise was far behind the cabin. From a safety standpoint, fuel lines and associated heat sources were located behind the cabin as well. From an aerodynamic point of view, engine thrust vectors were located much closer to the fuselage centerline than with wing-mounted engines, ensuring safer single-engine operations (should those occasions ever arise). Finally, an integral boarding stair was fitted to the lower fuselage aft of the rear pressure bulkhead, alleviating the need for cumbersome external boarding stairs at smaller airports.

To facilitate the airplane's development, the French physically grafted the sleek bullet-shaped nose of an existing jet airliner onto the forward barrel section of the Caravelle's fuselage. That other jetliner just happened to be Britain's de Havilland DH-106 Comet, recently grounded from a series of tragic inflight accidents (see Chapter Two). Sud purchased two complete nose sections from de Havilland and had them shipped from Hatfield, England, to Sud's final assembly facility at Toulouse. With the exception of engine pylons and tail surfaces built by Fiat in Genoa, Italy, the rest of the Caravelle's airframe was manufactured exclusively in France.

The first Caravelle prototype rolled out of Sud's final assembly building on April 21, 1955, and flew

successfully for the first time one month later. In November of that year, the country's national airline, Air France, placed an order for 12 Caravelles with 12 options, and the race was on. Certification flight testing was completed in March 1956, and route-proving and system-integration test flights soon began in earnest. One such flight offered a rather graphic demonstration of the aircraft's impressive single-engine performance when the second prototype flew between Paris and Casablanca on only one engine!

After the two prototypes, the Caravelle I became the first operational aircraft sporting a 3-foot fuselage stretch and a new avionics "hump" on the upper aft fuselage. Rolls-Royce Avon 522A engines provided 10,500 pounds of thrust each, and passenger capacity was established at 85 in an all-economy configuration. A slightly upgraded Caravelle 1A model was developed, after which the Caravelle III became the standard, with all earlier airplanes upgraded as IIIs. With a wingspan of 112 feet 6 inches and a fuselage length of 105 feet, the new jetliner was perfect for serving smaller outlying country airfields and big city airports alike.

Scandinavian Airlines System became the first airline in the Western world to inaugurate twin-engine pure-jet airliner service when it put the Caravelle III into operation flying from Copenhagen, Denmark, to Beirut, Lebanon, in April 1959. Air France began its Caravelle service on the Paris-Rome-Athens-Istanbul route the following month. Swissair and Air Algerie soon followed, flying the sleek twinjets on short- and medium-range routes throughout Europe and North Africa.

Other Caravelle III operators included Finnair, Alitalia, and Sabena in Europe, and Varig of Brazil in the Western hemisphere. A total of 111 Caravelle I, IA, and III models were built, while the total number of all Caravelles, including larger turbofan-powered versions, numbered 282 aircraft. This was the largest single production run of any European-built airliner at the time.

Tupolev Tu-104

In a new postwar era of escalating political, social, and technological competition, the Union of Soviet Socialist Republics was not about to be upstaged by its Western rivals when it came to the development of a jet-powered airliner. Adapting a military design for commercial passenger use had been a common theme since the first stodgy biplane transports of the 1920s, and Tupolev's new swept-wing, twinjet Tu-16 Badger medium bomber provided the perfect airframe from which to develop Russia's first jet airliner. This new transport would measure 121 feet long with a wingspan of 115 feet and would carry 50 passengers over routes of up to 1,800 miles. Its name would be the Tu-104.

The result of a post–World War II design study to re-establish France's proud aircraft industry, the Caravelle was the world's first jet aircraft to have its engines mounted on the rear fuselage, beginning the trend that has been adopted by numerous commercial aircraft and business jets alike. The Caravelle made its inaugural flight from Toulouse, France, in April 1955. (Mike Machat Collection)

THE FABULOUS FIFTIES
FLY ME TO THE MOON

EFFECTIVE JULY 1, 1955

TWA
TRANS WORLD AIRLINES
U.S.A. · EUROPE · AFRICA · ASIA

Fly TWA to
Disneyland
(see back cover)

FLY THE FINEST...
FLY TWA

TWA
30 YEARS
OF Service
1955

TWA Flight Schedule from July 1, 1955, seems to suggest that you could book your ticket for a TWA flight on either a Constellation from Los Angeles to New York, or a Moonliner from Los Angeles to the Moon and back! This clever marketing ploy actually established TWA as the official airline of Disneyland, which had just opened that same week. (Craig Kodera Collection)

"This is Captain Collins speaking," says the reassuring baritone voice over the ship's Public Address system. Our stewardess stands at the passenger door clad in the customary uniform of her airline, albeit a bit more futuristic. Everything bespeaks a typical passenger flight. Are we sitting onboard another TWA Constellation flight to New York? Hardly. We are comfortably seated in the passenger cabin of the *Star of Polaris* at Disneyland in Anaheim, California, in the fall of 1955, and this "spacecraft" is about to take us on a simulated flight to the moon!

Not just another ride at an amusement park, the TWA Moonliner in Tomorrowland acted as symbol and substance of the unlimited future world in twentieth-century America. There was absolutely no reason to believe we *couldn't* someday have revenue flights into space, just as we could most certainly count on robotically controlled houses and atomic flying cars in the not-to-distant years to come. Walt Disney, ever the visionary and (thankfully) the optimist, always knew to ask "why not?"

Designed by Disney Imagineer John Hench working under the tutelage of rocket scientists Wernher von Braun and Willy Ley, the 76-foot-tall "Rocket to the Moon," as it was officially known, was actually a one-third-scale model of the real spacecraft envisioned by its creators. The rocket was clad in aluminum sheeting, just like the real thing, although it was structurally like a boiler with its steel skeleton. Early in the planning process as part of Disney's sense of dynamic marketing, Ralph Damon, president of TWA, was brought into the mix so that the red stripes of Trans World Airlines would be seen flying over the park. A nice touch of believability for Disney, the advertising for the airline was beyond effective. After all, TWA at that time was the official air carrier of Disneyland. As an added bonus, Disney struck another deal, this time with StromBecKer Models to recreate plastic kits of several items from park rides, most notably, the Moonliner. You could purchase one of these kits only a few yards from the real thing, in what was known as Hobbyland, and the new concept of "cross marketing" was born.

Inside the attraction itself, passengers with their mock boarding passes proceeded to a terminal boarding area clad with TWA signage and staging. Here they viewed a TWA "agent" explaining the workings of their rocket and the trip into space using a cutaway model, plus animated films on the space-port viewing screens. All reference to dates was the year 1986. Inside the passenger compartment now, two more gigantic viewing screens, one above and one below, showed all aspects of our flight. The ever-present voice of Captain Collins, as he narrated our progress and provided scientific knowledge and perspective, reassured us that all this spaceflight business was purely routine and that we would return safely to our launching port unscathed. Passengers on the ride enjoyed the earliest use of air jackhammers and moving seats to heighten the effects and impart realism to the movement and motion of the rocket. This truly was a realistic look at spaceflight, as far as thinking in 1955 went.

Coincident with this attraction, the Disney television program seen on Sunday nights featured a three-part series inspired by a multipart serial in *Collier's* magazine, using live actors and plenty of animation. Titled "Man In Space," one episode borrowed portions of the presentation from the Rocket to the Moon ride at the park. In short, everywhere one looked in the mid-1950s, space exploration was an integral part of our adventure through life. This tugged at the more sobering reality of flying a prop-driven airliner to span the country, which therefore became preparatory to understanding why the future *must* include commercial jet transports. In the meantime, however, flying to the moon on TWA was just about the most "futuramic" thing a regular person could do.

Another bright, sunny day in Southern California helps to highlight the futuristic shape of TWA's Moonliner at Disneyland's "Tomorrowland." (www.davelandweb.com)

Powered by two Mikulin AM-3 turbojets producing 17,640 pounds of thrust each, the prototype Tu-104 took to the Russian skies for the first time on June 17, 1955. Because so much of Soviet development was shrouded in secrecy behind what the world called "The Iron Curtain," the Tu-104's first appearance at London's Heathrow Airport in March 1956 literally caught the world off guard. While this surprise happenstance was indeed a benchmark in heralding Russia's presence as a world power, the Soviets upped the ante one year later by placing *Sputnik*, the world's first man-made satellite, into orbit around the Earth. This single event radically changed the balance of technological power and launched the Space Race that eventually landed men on the moon and produced today's International Space Station. (See sidebar "The Fabulous Fifties: Fly Me to the Moon," page 71.)

By 1959, Aeroflot, Russia's national airline, had inaugurated Tu-104 service from Moscow to a host of European cities such as London, Paris, Brussels, Prague, Amsterdam, and Copenhagen. In the mother country, Aeroflot's Tu-104s (and improved 70-passenger Tu-104As) were plying routes between Moscow, Leningrad, and Kiev in the west, and cities as far east as Vladivostok. International Tu-104 destinations included Cairo, Delhi, Peking, and Pyongyang, although all of the longer-range flights included intermediate stops.

With its cruising speed of 495 mph and passenger capacity of half the later four-engined jetliners, the hefty 160,000-pound Tu-104 will have to be judged by historians as a vital step in the development of the jet airliner rather than a groundbreaking revolutionary design that set the bar for today's impressive jet fleets. However, those same historians would also have to note that the Tupolev Tu-104 was, in reality, the world's first jet airliner to conduct sustained-revenue passenger operations after the loss of the de Havilland Comet 1s in 1954.

Having entered service in September 1956 and flying continuously until its retirement in 1981, the Tu-104 established an enviable record for safety and reliability for nearly a quarter-century. (This mark is even more impressive considering the severity of the Soviet winter environment.) In final judgment, the sleek twinjet with the distinctive glass bombardier nose section will always be remembered as the aircraft that put Soviet commercial jet operations on the world map.

A commercial adaptation of the Soviet Air Force Tupolev Tu-16 Badger bomber, the Tu-104 was the Soviet Union's first jet airliner, and entered into commercial service before either of America's first two jetliners, the 707 and DC-8, had even flown. (Mike Machat Collection)

Chapter Six

ZENITH OF THE PROPLINERS
(1956-1958)

Northwest Passage, *a Northwest Orient Airlines Douglas DC-7C in 1957, by Craig Kodera.* (Craig Kodera)

With the Jet Age looming ever closer, piston-powered airliners reach the absolute peak of their development. Nonstop intercontinental air travel has now become routine, and slick, colorful ads for luxurious commercial air transportation permeate the mass media. Ironically, the peak of propliner development also represents the absolute limit of their development, as air carriers and the traveling public prepare for the next big step.

Airliner Order Book and Impending Swan Song for the Pistons

In September 1958, the Air Transport Association (ATA) completed a survey of airline orders for new turboprop and turbojet commercial airliners covering the period from 1958 through 1962. First revealed to the public in the January 1959 issue of *FLYING* magazine, these orders served as a veritable scorecard for the coming passenger Jet Age lurking just over the horizon. U.S. airlines held orders for 179 turboprop and 309 turbojet aircraft, while foreign carriers were shown to have orders for 264 turboprops and 245 turbojets, bringing the grand total to 997 turbine-powered airliners by 1962. This meant that 11 different manufacturers would build nearly 1,000 brand-new airliners in the first four years of the commercial Jet Age.

Breaking that scorecard down by individual aircraft type, we can see an even clearer indication of which manufacturing companies were at the top of their game:

Aircraft Type	U.S. Orders	Foreign Orders	Total Orders
Boeing 707	94	68	162
Boeing 720	36	0	36
Douglas DC-8	105	40	145
Convair 880	49*	13	62
Convair 990	25	0	25
Lockheed L-188	129	33	162
Fairchild F-27	36	19	55
Vickers Viscount	75	109	184
de Havilland Comet IV	0	32	32
Sud Caravelle	0	49	49
Tupolev Tu-104	0	40**	40
Bristol Britannia	0	22	22
Vickers Vanguard	0	40	40
Fokker Friendship (F-27)	0	41	41

* Includes nine aircraft ordered by, but never delivered to, Capital Airlines.
** Number was approximate at the time and does not include provisional orders for the Tu-114.

Further examination of the above chart shows some very interesting facts. For instance, in 1958 America's most popular new airliners were the Boeing 707 and Lockheed Electra with 162 orders each through the end of 1962. Next would be the Douglas DC-8 (145), with the Convair 880 coming in a distant third (62). It is also interesting to note that although no foreign pure-jet transports were on order from U.S. airlines at the time of the survey, United Air Lines contracted for 20 French Caravelles shortly after this survey was completed.

As we will see, the total orders for all the above-named aircraft increased rather dramatically over their life spans, but judging an aircraft type's success by looking at these numbers is not unlike looking at the odds for racehorses just as they are preparing to leave the gate. What is even more telling is that by the time these orders were placed, the final and penultimate models of both the Douglas DC-7 and Lockheed Constellation had already been flying for three years. Once the new jets entered service, however, the age of the large, long-range, propeller-driven airliner as the primary means of worldwide commercial air transportation ended almost immediately.

Preparing for the Jets

By this point, in the mid-1950s, excitement and anticipation for the coming jets was rising to a fever pitch. The mass media was awash in colorful ads touting the new generation of jet airliners about to take to the skies. You couldn't pick up a copy of *Reader's Digest*, *National Geographic*, *LIFE*, *Look*, or *Collier's* without seeing myriad ads from Boeing, Douglas, and Convair extolling the exciting virtues of commercial jet travel. Images usually included swept-wing shapes with white contrails against a dark blue sky, and maybe even a full moon thrown in for dramatic effect. A smooth ride, quietness, and above all, speed, were always the featured highlights of these ads with lots of young kids shown gazing wide-eyed at tall, handsome airline captains and their new jets.

From an operational standpoint, however, airline and airport managers were grappling with the unknown. Although both Los Angeles and New York had plans for big jetports on the drawing board in 1955 for LAX and Idlewild, both facilities were still years away from having 10,000-foot-long runways, modern roomy terminals with fully enclosed jet bridges, and acres of bright new concrete ramp space. Airline planners were trying to cope with how they could best integrate the monstrous smoke-spewing jets among tightly grouped DC-6s, -7s, Connies, and Convairs parked next to a terminal building like so many cattle waiting in a stockyard. The jets' larger wingspans and exhaust blasts alone were cause for concern, and soon, contingency plans were formulated to park and service the jetliners at the very end of boarding concourses, safely away from the prop aircraft, if for nothing else, ease of operations.

Yes, the promise of swift five-hour coast-to-coast flights and luxury travel in the stratosphere was certainly enticing to the traveling public and aircraft enthusiasts alike. However, the cold prickly reality of how to incorporate these fire-breathing machines with their passenger loads of twice the norm into existing airport infrastructure was daunting. In studying the specific problems the new jets would represent, it was quite evident that a

NOW IN SERVICE!

The largest and most luxurious airliner ever built!

TWA JETSTREAM*

There's nothing like it in the sky! This magnificent Lockheed Starliner, the largest and longest-range transport of them all, flies high above the weather, can even reach and ride the swift winds of the jet stream. With exclusive synchrophased (anti-vibration) propellers, with engines placed far out on the wings, the Jetstream offers you the *quietest* coast-to-coast and trans-Atlantic trip in history. Welcome aboard!

RESERVE NOW! Non-stop between New York and California, non-stop from New York to London/Paris. See your nearby travel agent, your local TWA ticket office or write TWA at 380 Madison Avenue, New York 17, New York. *Jetstream is a service mark owned exclusively by TWA.*

FLY THE FINEST

FLY TWA
TRANS WORLD AIRLINES

© Trans World Airlines, Inc.

As anticipation for the next generation of transports continued to build with the traveling public in the mid-1950s, just using the word "jet" somehow seemed to bring the new air age closer. Enter the Jetstream Constellation in 1957, better known as Lockheed's Model 1649A Starliner. Los Angeles illustration icon Ren Wicks worked for Howard Hughes painting everything from movie posters to airline ads. For this 1649 image, Hughes specifically asked him to exaggerate the aircraft's wingspan and distance of the engines outboard from the fuselage. Here is the result! (Mike Machat Collection)

new paradigm in airport design and aircraft operations would be required to cope with the pending onslaught of new commercial jetliners. Until that happened, however, jets and props would have to be operated in a "best of both worlds" environment. To paraphrase the famous line from Dickens, "It was the best of times" for the final generation of propliners, and "the worst of times" realizing the jets were coming, and not being quite ready to cope with the expected changes.

Aircraft of the Era

"Zenith" is defined by Webster's Dictionary as "the highest point reached...by a celestial body." However, in the context of piston-powered airliners built by the Douglas and Lockheed Aircraft Companies, that word would have to be defined by the DC-7C and 1649 Constellation, respectively.

Douglas DC-7C Seven Seas

Successfully meeting specific airline requirements was the name of the game for aircraft manufacturers in the 1950s. To satisfy Pan American's need for an extended-range aircraft capable of flying the Atlantic nonstop in either direction despite prevailing winds, Douglas engineers once again rose to the challenge by combining the DC-7B's uprated engines and increased fuel capacity with a slightly larger airframe. The result was the stunning DC-7, named "Seven Seas" to denote the area of the Earth's surface that it could reach, as well as a clever play on words for its alpha-numeric designation.

Structural enhancements included a 4-foot fuselage stretch by adding one window ahead of the wing, a 10-foot-wider wingspan achieved by inserting constant-

chord plugs at the wing roots, a finer-ratio radar nose contour, and a 3-foot-taller vertical stabilizer for better yaw control to compensate for the aircraft's longer fuselage and wider engine placement on the wings. Additional advantages of the enhanced wingspan were a quieter cabin resulting from the inboard engines being placed 5 feet farther away from the fuselage, and a wider track for the aircraft's main landing gear. This latter feature allowed softer landing touchdowns for passengers and better ground handling for pilots.

First flown on December 20, 1955, the -7C immediately captured the flying public's imagination as the

Seen parked on the west ramp at Douglas' Santa Monica, California, facility, this rear-three-quarter view of the DC-7C gives a good indication of the taller, vertical stabilizer and extended constant-chord wing-root section. Evident also are the extended-range "saddle" fuel tanks added to the top rear of each engine nacelle. (Craig Kodera Collection)

Looking somewhat reminiscent of the TWA Jetstream ad (on page 75), here is Douglas Aircraft Company's answer to the Lockheed 1649. Using similar design philosophies to extend the wingspan, move the engines farther outboard, and create the ultimate version of the series, Douglas engineers designed the largest and longest-range DC-7 ever. The name Seven Seas was not only a play on words for the DC-7C designation, but it called attention to the fact that this new airliner was easily capable of spanning the seven seas. (Mike Machat Collection)

ultimate propeller-driven airliner. This elegant airplane entered commercial service with Pan American on June 1, 1956; European customers Swissair, SAS, Alitalia, Sabena, BOAC, and KLM soon followed suit. Braniff International was able to capitalize on the new aircraft's stellar performance with its South American routes, flying such never-before-possible stage lengths as New York-to-Rio de Janeiro nonstop. In the Pacific region, Northwest Orient and Japan Air Lines both used their Seven Seas for flights from the U.S. West Coast to points throughout Eastern Asia.

The DC-7C's Wright R-3350-18EA turbo-compound engines provided 30-percent more power on takeoff than the R-3350s that powered the DC-7, but these powerplants were marvels of modern engineering and a plumber's nightmare at the same time. Capable of producing 3,400 hp each, these 18-cylinder monsters were initially developed for Lockheed's P2V Neptune Navy Patrol Bomber. unfortunately, problems associated with their sheer complexity were soon having an impact on the DC-7C's operational reliability, and by 1958 the airplane's pilots, passengers, and maintenance personnel were longing for the simplicity and reliability of the older DC-6B's Pratt & Whitney R-2800 Double Wasps.

Like the long-range version of the DC-7B, the -7C carried supplemental fuel in its engine nacelle saddle tanks, but an additional 1,000-gallon wing center section tank gave this new aircraft a total capacity of 7,825 gallons, easily allowing flights of nearly 5,000 miles in distance and up to 18 hours in duration. Maximum gross takeoff weight jumped from the DC-7's 122,000 pounds to 143,000 pounds, but the true advantage gained was the Seven Seas' impressive cruising speed of 350 mph and top speed of 410 mph. Used in front-line service for less than five years, the DC-7C was still the undisputed "King of the Hill" of Douglas piston-powered airliners. The final airframe of 121 DC-7Cs was delivered to KLM Royal Dutch Airlines in December 1958—two months after the Boeing 707 was first introduced into service.

Lockheed 1649A Constellation

As we've seen, the Douglas-Lockheed rivalry seemed to ratchet-up with every single version of the DC-6/DC-7 series versus the Constellation. The DC-7C would prove to be no different, with the Santa Monica-based company seemingly throwing down the gauntlet for the "Boys from Burbank" to come up with something better, and indeed—in some ways, at least—they did.

This photograph of the Lockheed Starliner banking away from the camera plane clearly shows the wing's razor-straight leading and trailing edges, and the fact that the 1649A's wingspan actually exceeded its length. We can also easily see that the wing root is located approximately 3 feet farther aft on the fuselage than the 1049G configuration that preceded it. (TWA/Jon Proctor Collection)

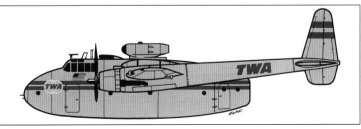

In order to deliver replacement engines to TWA airliners stranded at stops along the airline's overseas routes, a modified post–World War II–vintage Fairchild C-82 Packet named Ontos was put into service in 1957. Beginning with Wright R-3350 turbo-compound radial powerplants and then delivering turbojet engines into the early 1970s as well, this C-82's performance was augmented with a single 3,250-pound-thrust Westinghouse J34 jet engine mounted on a pylon above the fuselage. (Mike Machat)

San Francisco Airport, October 2, 1957: TWA inaugural Polar Flight 801 sits on the ramp following its record-breaking 23-hour 19-minute nonstop flight from London. Amazingly, the same augmented cockpit crew operated the flight on to Los Angeles, its final destination. (Harry Sievers)

The model 1649A's wingspan exceeded its length, as can be seen in this March 1958 photograph, taken at the New York–Idlewild's International Arrivals Building. (Harry Sievers)

Called the 1649A Starliner, this ultimate version of the Connie proved to be one of the most visually striking airliners ever built. Although the fuselage was identical to the stretched 1049G, the classic curves of the previous P-38-style tapered-wing planform gave way to razor-straight leading and trailing edges, providing the 1649A with a 150-foot span and the highest-aspect-ratio wing of any piston-powered airliner. Like the DC-7C, the Starliner's engines were moved outboard by 5 feet, providing lower cabin noise levels, less vibration, and a wider main landing gear track. Maximum gross takeoff weight jumped to 160,000 pounds, a 17,000-pound advantage over the Seven Seas, although the 1649A's cruising speed was considerably slower at a stately 290 mph.

The Wright R-3350-18EA turbo-compounds were also the same on both aircraft, and a desirable byproduct of the turbo-compressor was that the engine exhaust was relatively cool by the time it exited the massive pipes on either side of the nacelle. Gone were the days of passengers near the wing being able to read their newspapers at night solely by the light of flames belching out of engine exhausts at cruise power. Larger-diameter three-bladed props capped by longer propeller spinners were also added on the 1649A.

Unfortunately, the reliability of the 1649A's powerplants also matched that of the -7C, but the ever-innovative TWA came up with a unique plan to cope with that problem. A military-surplus Fairchild C-82 Packet affectionately named *Ontos* (the Greek word for "thing") was added to the airline's fleet in 1957 specifically to carry new or spare engines to outlying TWA cities in the event a Starliner sat stranded with engine

Before lowering your tray tables became the standard fare for inflight dining, placing a thin plastic tray of hot food on a pillow in your lap was the traditional method. Looking at this photo of a 1649A interior, one can't help but wonder where the hot coffee in the flight attendant's coffee pot is about to go. Note drawn curtains on the windows. (Craig Kodera Collection)

problems. It later served in this same role carrying spare jet engines for TWA's 707s and even jumbo 747s before being retired in January 1972. The C-82, built originally in 1948 to carry cargo or paratroopers, was a small twin-engine, twin-tailboom aircraft that was modified with the addition of a single Westinghouse J34 turbojet mounted in a pod above the fuselage to augment the freight hauler's sluggish takeoff performance at maximum gross weight.

TWA inaugurated 1649A "Jetstream" service on June 1, 1957, exactly one year to the day later than the DC-7C. Its massive wing held 9,600 gallons of fuel, giving the aircraft a 5,500-mile maximum range that was 600 miles longer than the -7C's. This capability enabled nonstop flights from Europe westbound to Los Angeles or San Francisco via the polar route. The inaugural flight from London to San Francisco took a record 23 hours 19 minutes when a TWA Jetstream encountered formidable headwinds en route.

As majestic an airliner as the 1649A was in 1957, few airlines had the specific passenger and range requirements to make the Starliner a viable addition to their fleets, although Air France, Lufthansa, and launch customer TWA were proud operators of the type through the end of the decade. A number of Starliners enjoyed a brief afterlife in the long-range freighter role, but the airplane lasted less than three years in front-line service. The last of only 44 Starliners built was delivered to Trans World Airlines in June 1958.

With longer-range versions of the new Boeing 707 and Douglas DC-8 jetliners entering service by 1960, the final nails were driven into the proverbial coffins of both the Seven Seas and the Starliner as the world's flagship airliners, proving that sometimes in aviation, the ultimate development of an aircraft type can be simply too much, too late.

Vickers Viscount

Whenever a new technology is introduced, there is always the inevitable first and best model, or brand, or demonstrator. In the new postwar world of turbine-propeller aviation, the Vickers Viscount was that leader, and the one to beat.

In answer to the Brabazon Committee's 2B outline request for a commercial transport capable of carrying 24 passengers at 280 mph over a distance of 700 miles, Vickers responded with a proposal called the VC-2 Viceroy. This design used four of the new Rolls-Royce Dart engines, and after BEA took a strong interest in the concept, the capacity was increased to 32 passengers. The prototype airplane was known as the 630, and its first flight took place in July 1948.

The prototype was seen absolutely everywhere, at first showing off at the Farnborough displays, commonly flying with three of four engines shut down, then after its type certificate was granted in 1950, official sales tours and proving flights were initiated.

As the capabilities of the Dart engine grew, so did the Viscount. (The name Viscount was exchanged for Viceroy after the independence of India from the British Empire.) Employing the new Dart RDa3 Mark 504 powerplant in the 700-series airplane, the 50-percent increase in power allowed the fuselage to be lengthened by 6 feet 8 inches, and the wingspan to increase by nearly 5 feet. First flight took place on August 28, 1950. The range of this larger aircraft was now nearly 1,000 miles. The passenger load increased once again, this time to somewhere between 40 and 53 seats, and this ultimately refined design was now the production standard with which to begin the Viscount assembly line.

Airline passenger service first began with BEA and a 701-series Viscount on April 18, 1953, on a flight from London Heathrow to Rome, Athens, and Nicosia. Because the last leg was under contract to Cyprus Airways, that line holds the distinction of being second in the world to carry passengers on a Viscount. Even as this new groundbreaking service was starting, just a few days prior BEA had signed a contract for the new, larger Viscount 802, capable of carrying 70 passengers at 325 mph.

Considerable interest for or about the Viscount was also stirring in North American airline boardrooms, and to satisfy the regulatory bodies of Canada and America, Vickers drew up the 724-series airplane. Capital Airlines immediately ordered 60 airplanes, an absolutely gigantic number in 1954! This then became the production standard airframe and was known in general as the 700D. The D model had Dart 510 engines. Capital introduced the Viscount to passengers in the United States in July 1955. Trans-Canada Air Lines, which operated 34 of the new turboprops, holds the honor of making the first Viscount flights in North America by virtue of beginning service on April 1, 1955.

By 1956, more than 200 Viscounts had been ordered. The British finally had a world-beater airliner design, which was selling beyond wildest expectations. Passenger acceptance was off the charts as well, what with the fast, smooth, and fairly quiet behavior of this airplane. The large vertical oval windows were part of the joy of flying in a Viscount, as one could see everything!

In short, the Viscount was indeed a truly stunning development within the airline world. Capitalizing on that success, Vickers made the seemingly inevitable decision to stretch the airframe. As mentioned above, BEA was the instigator for a higher-capacity airplane, and initially liked the 801 series, which was a whopping 13 feet longer than the 700 and could carry up to 86 fares. Sober consideration prevailed, and the 802 was born to take the place of the 801, with a mere 46-inch extension of the fuselage. Moving the fore and aft bulkheads allowed for the large increase of cabin space, in spite of the small external stretch, and 68 of these airplanes wound up being delivered to six carriers.

Although the 802 was a simple stretch of the 700, which meant more passengers over a shorter or same distance, the final Viscount type, the 810, really was the penultimate development of the design. The same size as the other 800 airplanes, the 810 was matched up with the new Dart 525 engines, which allowed for an

As Great Britain was the first with a turbojet-powered transport, so it was again with the world's first production turboprop transport—the inimitable Vickers Viscount. Although smaller than the Lockheed Electra that would come later, the Viscount entered service with BEA in 1953 and brought the advantages of faster and smoother turbine power to the world's airlines well before the big jets later in that decade. (Vickers/Mike Machat Collection)

Capital Airlines became the first Viscount operator in the United States, flying more than 60 of the type from 1955 until its merger with United Air Lines six years later. The forty-second airplane was delivered from Vickers' Weybridge, England, factory in September 1956. The new turboprop was a solid hit with passengers when it first entered service, despite the shrill note of its Rolls-Royce Dart engines. (Jon Proctor Collection)

Viscount 812s began joining Continental Airlines' inventory in May 1958, building to a fleet of 15 Viscounts by mid 1959. The airline's ninth example, N248V, is seen here on display at the Farnborough Airshow in September 1958. Note Fairey Rotodyne at right. (Jon Proctor Collection)

impressive 17-percent increase in maximum gross take-off weight. This then translated into nearly doubling the aircraft's range—and now the Viscount really had something to it.

In the United States, the premier operator of the final version was Continental Airlines. It started commercial operations in May 1958, and owned 15 Viscounts. Overseas, it was Lufthansa and Austrian flying the 810, among several other airlines worldwide. When all was said and done, with the last delivery of a Viscount to China's CAAC in 1964, the airplane carried the distinction of being Britain's most successful airliner in terms of number built and sold. Final score: 60 operators in 40 different countries, and more than 150 second-hand operators as well.

Bristol Britannia

The Bristol Britannia was one of the great short-fall stories of British commercial aviation. It was an airplane with so much promise, but a case of bad breaks and ultimately poor timing nipped this beautiful airliner in the bud.

Beginning life as the chosen design to satisfy the Brabazon Committee's Type 3 airline transport, the original series 100 Britannia was far different than the production machine. The initial design only needed to meet the requirement for 1,500-miles range and around 32 passengers. As with everything in the postwar period the airframe grew until the type was redesigned for

BOAC to "175 standard," which translated to carrying 90 passengers over 2,740 mile.

Another crucial and fateful design change was made prior to the first metal being cut: replacing the Centaurus piston engines with Bristol's Proteus *turbo-prop* powerplants. Herein lay the diminution of the Britannia as the years passed.

First flight of the aircraft took place in August 1952 with a 101-series airplane. One other prototype flew in December 1953, and the first airline service began on February 1, 1957. (We mention the beginning and ending numbers to highlight the enormous lag time until service entry.) The flight-test program was dogged by a few problems, but most notably, the Proteus engines were completely unreliable and prone to an unusual icing condition, which would, in eventual progression, "suffocate" the engines and lead to inflight shutdowns. The problem was eventually diagnosed and a suitable fix was designed, but much valuable time had been lost in the interim.

Originally anticipating a large swell of orders from the world's major airlines, Bristol contracted with Short Brothers in Belfast, Northern Ireland, to utilize their production facilities as a second assembly line. As the engine problems dragged on this became less a necessity, but the 250 series was built on that line with a forward cargo door and a standard load of passengers aft.

The late-development series of the airplane was the 300. Sporting a longer fuselage with greater range, the

The only North American customer to operate Bristol's magnificent Britannia was Canadian Pacific, which used the type on its long-haul Pacific flights. Empress of Vancouver *is seen here at its namesake airport.* (Mel Lawrence)

The Canadian-built CL-44 served with Flying Tiger Line, as evidenced by N229SW, which was acquired in a merger with Seaboard & Western. A novel feature of this Britannia variant was the swing tail that opened 90 degrees for rear fuselage cargo loading and unloading. (via Paul Nowaske)

"Big Britannia" could now carry 114 passengers over a huge 4,100-mile range. BOAC flew the 312 on routes that included London Heathrow to New York, but the airline eventually encircled the globe with its fleet of Britannias. Canadian Pacific and El Al also utilized the 310 Britannia with its long intercontinental legs.

Perhaps two of the most fascinating Britannia airline orders that never materialized were from Capital and Northeast. Both were avid Viscount operators that needed additional passenger carriage and nonstop range for their premier routes and, therefore, looked to the British and their lead in turbine-propeller development for the answer. The Britannia fit the bill perfectly: long range and high capacity in the 300, and a luxurious ride

to boot! Bristol produced the first aircraft for both carriers, even painting the airliners in each company's respective colors, with the Northeast airplane looking especially stunning in its midnight-blue-and-white livery. But for reasons of financial health and the cold reality of the Britannia simply being the wrong aircraft for those airlines at that particular time, the orders were canceled and the airplanes were placed with other carriers.

The Bristol Britannia was known as "The Whispering Giant," and the name was quite apt. This elegant and efficient airplane might have reached a great pinnacle in airline history, but alas, fate was just not kind to the big, graceful airplane from Filton. Only a mere 85 Britannias were built.

TRAVELING IN STYLE
TWA's AMBASSADOR SERVICE

The zenith of luxury during the golden age of propliners was TWA's nonstop Polar service between California and Europe aboard the Lockheed 1649A Jetstream. Ambassador Flight 870 appears ready to accept passengers at Los Angeles for its flight to Paris. (Mel Lawrence)

Faced with serious postwar competition from irregular, non-scheduled airlines, U.S. trunk carriers struck back with what became known as "tourist" or "coach" service, implemented using higher-density seating or standard-configuration airplanes at off-peak hours; what many purists considered the beginning of the end of civilized air travel. Most of these flights featured boxed meals available for purchase in the airport terminal before boarding, multiple en-route stops, and long rides in cramped cabins.

Sleeping berths, a more common feature on pre-war aircraft, began to disappear with the advent of faster, four-engine equipment. In the United States, American Airlines and TWA retained berths on new DC-6s and Constellations for added comfort on longer domestic segments, as did United for its Hawaii service. But gradually, sleeping accommoda-

tions were removed from the Douglas types. Meanwhile, TWA's transatlantic routes justified the berths and gave it an advantage on its longest flights within North America. At the same time, airline managers recognized the demand for premium service above and beyond standard first class.

In 1948, just a year before TWA began offering Sky Coach flights within the United States, the airline took its transatlantic service to a higher level by introducing weekly, all-sleeper "Paris Sky Chief" flights between New York and Paris with a scheduled stop at Gander; westbound, it became the "New York Sky Chief." Limited to only 18 passengers, the cabin layout included a cocktail lounge in the forward section of the main cabin. Advertisements spoke of champagne dinners and a pre-arrival hot breakfast "served in bed, if you prefer!" With the delivery of longer-range

Flying in the lap of luxury at 25,000 feet, well-dressed passengers enjoy the sumptuous dining pleasures of TWA's Ambassador Service aboard a Lockheed 1049G Super-G Constellation. (Craig Kodera Collection)

749A Connies, TWA moved these trips from LaGuardia to the newer Idlewild Airport with its longer runways, beginning nonstop flights in November 1951, although weather conditions still dictated occasional en-route landings for fuel.

The upgraded flights became known as Paris and New York "International Ambassador Service," while the Sky Chief name was reassigned to domestic first-class segments. A similar service was initiated with TWA's new New York-to-London route, and sleeper flights were increased to twice-weekly frequencies.

The Ambassador name was carried over to domestic service with TWA's introduction of 1049 Super Constellations, referred to as "Ambassador Service in the U.S." Although restricted to domestic flights, the 64-seat, all-first-class Super Connie cabins were equipped with eight convertible berths for use on night flights. A fold-down table in the "cozy" seven-seat lounge provided space for an elaborate snack buffet presentation.

Ambassador Service was greatly enhanced with the introduction of 1049G Super G Constellations in

September 1956, the first dual-class aircraft in the United States. Passengers seated in the noisier forward cabin received "Golden Banner Deluxe Coach Service" that featured hot meals for purchase, along with cocktails for sale. Meanwhile, a limited number of sleeping berths were available for Ambassador customers on night flights. In the more spacious mid-cabin "Mural Lounge," canapés were offered from a silver serving tray, along with cocktails before an elaborate meal service with wine and champagne.

The ultimate Ambassador Service was offered aboard TWA's Model 1649A Starliners, which were referred to as "Jetstreams," a reference to the fact that the airplane could take advantage of high-altitude jet-stream winds, although the clever deception came from the reference to jets that were yet to arrive. TWA even featured illustrations of the airplane in its advertising, sans propellers, a tactic discontinued after a storm of protests from competing airlines. This airplane, often referred to as the "Cadillac" of the Constellation series, entered service with TWA in June 1957 on transatlantic and longer domestic routes.

The airline's 1649As were furnished with "Siesta Sleeper Seats," perhaps the most comfortable on any airliner at the time. With pull-out footrests and deep seatback recline, the chairs were nearly as comfortable as the sleeper berths that were also available, and provided a competitive edge, both on transatlantic and transcontinental segments. In the Mural Lounges, each 1649A featured a different colorful Maric Zamparelli wall painting representing major cities and nations served by TWA.

Perhaps the Jetstream's greatest asset was its ability to provide reliable nonstop flights across the Atlantic in both directions, even from southern Europe. Its range was sufficient enough to allow TWA to begin nonstop flights between U.S. West Coast cities and Europe via the polar route. And while Super G Connies and DC-7s struggled to complete westbound nonstop routes across the country against heavy winter winds, the Jetstream flew these segments with ease.

The Ambassador moniker gave way to TWA's "Royal Ambassador Service" in June 1961, aboard Boeing 707s across the Atlantic. Perhaps the ultimate first-class experience at the time, it was limited to just 20 passengers and began with hand luggage delivered to the passenger's reserved seat. A choice of seven dinner entrees included Chateaubriand carved on an aisle cart, part of a multi-course, 2½-hour meal presentation. "R/A Service," as it was known within the airline industry, was later expanded to long-haul domestic flights and became the envy of competing airlines for the rest of the decade.

In April 1970, TWA resurrected the Ambassador Service trademark as part of a complete makeover of its Boeing 707 and Convair 880 cabin interiors to more closely match the 747s that began joining the fleet earlier in the year. The identity, which extended to both first class and coach, later expanded to the airline's 727s as well.

Although the "new" Ambassador Service was well received, it could not match the individualized attention that cabin crews were able to give their customers on the longer flights of the pre-jet era, when there was time for leisurely meals, making up sleeping berths, and offering passengers breakfast in bed.

This aft-looking picture shows TWA's luxurious 1649A Jetstream first-class "Starlight Lounge." Artist Maric Zamparelli was commissioned to create murals representing different cities and countries served by the airline, to adorn the lounge-cabin sidewall. (TWA/Jon Proctor Collection)

Chapter Seven

CHANGING OF THE GUARD
(1958-1960)

Darts Over The Hudson. *Viscount Airlines' Vickers Viscount over Manhattan in 1958.* (Craig Kodera)

The age of turbine-powered commercial aircraft officially begins with new foreign-built turboprop regional airliners replacing the stalwart piston-powered transports of the time. Although the world's first-generation jetliners are making their appearance, they are still months away from certification for passenger use. The airline industry is preparing for an impending change as the world awaits the beginning of an exciting new era in travel.

"Jet Powered"

If you lived in Small Town, USA, in 1958 and were worried that the jet revolution would pass you by, you shouldn't have been. The local service carriers that supported such cities with airline service had a big surprise for customers, with airplanes like the twin-turboprop Fairchild F-27. Whether for business or family trips, the wonder of turbine aviation in the late-1950s was a breath of fresh air for communities with travelers tired and beat-up from flying on what seemed like "ancient," stuffy, old DC-3s. On route segments to larger cities, the four-engine Vickers Viscount brought turbine-

powered flight to modern commercial aviation, and the Bristol Britannia ruled the transoceanic skies.

Turboprops were exciting: the sounds, the smell of kerosene, the speed. There was an overall impressiveness

WELCOME ABOARD THE VISCOUNT

By Mike Machat

The businessman from Hartford and veteran airline traveler boarded the stairs and stepped through the oval door of the brand-new, factory-fresh red-and-white Capital Airlines Viscount parked on the ramp at Newark Airport. Strapping into his seat, he noticed the size of the window—about twice that of the Constellations he was used to flying in, and oval as well. As the slim, four-bladed Dowty-Rotol propellers started turning, the familiar smoky, coughing engines start and piston-induced vibrations he usually felt at this moment were replaced by almost complete silence and a new smooth hum. Then the rising note of turbine whine

slowly grew into a shrieking cacophony emanating from the aircraft's slim nacelles housing its four Rolls-Royce Darts.

Acceleration on takeoff was dazzling by comparison to a DC-7 or a Constellation, but with a stately 315-mph cruise speed, actual times en route were not all that different from the Viscount's piston-powered counterparts. The flying experience itself, however, was another story, for the ride was noticeably smoother, it was quieter inside the cabin, and the trip was less fatiguing. Although not as fast or as large as the soon-to-come turboprop Electra from Lockheed and the Bristol Britannia from England, the Viscount nevertheless set the stage for the age of turbine-powered regional-service air travel.

United Air Lines retained a large Viscount fleet after the 1961 merger with Capital and kept the type in service through the end of the decade. N7428 is pictured here awaiting its passengers on a brief stopover at Grand Rapids, Michigan, in 1968. (Thomas Livesey Collection)

about them, and an importance to the use of this new powerplant that changed commercial aviation forever. The turbine engine now connected Main Street in your town, to the bustling thoroughfares of big city America and beyond.

Turboprops in Airline Service

Until Viscount 800s began flying with Continental Airlines on May 28, 1958, turboprop airliner service within the United States was limited to points east of the Mississippi River, where Viscount 700s flew in the colors of Capital Airlines, which assured the type's success with a massive order for 60 airplanes. From north of the border, Trans-Canada Air Lines brought its Viscounts into airports at Boston, New York, Detroit, Chicago, and Seattle.

Based at Boston, quasi-regional-carrier Northeast Airlines took a small fleet of 10 Viscount 700s in lieu of a failed Bristol Britannia order, and enjoyed competitive

Passengers board a British European Airways Vanguard for a short-haul European flight. (Allan Van Wickler)

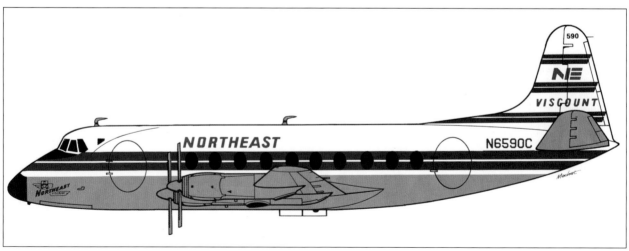

Northeast Airlines operated the 700-series Viscounts on its East Coast routes as far south as Washington, D.C. Northeast's was a particularly smart-looking color scheme for this airplane. (Mike Machat)

success with the type on shorter segments, including the dense Boston–New York–Washington commuter run. This then was the immediate Jet Age effect that the turboprop had on routes and passengers wherever the airplanes flew.

Its capacity on a par with the Convair 340 and 440, the Viscount distinguished itself with its speed and quieter interior noise level, while at airports its shrill whine was a familiar nuisance. Like the Capital, Northeast, and Trans-Canada turboprops, Continental's larger, 56-seat Viscount II was all-first-class configured and advertised as "First in the West with Jet Power Flights," operating between Chicago and Los Angeles with stops at Kansas City and/or Denver beginning May 28, 1958. Meanwhile, Club Coach DC-7Bs handled the Chicago-Los Angeles nonstops until Boeing 707s replaced the type in 1959. Viscount II service was later expanded to routes in Texas and across the southwestern tier of states.

The Fairchild-built F-27 started flying with West Coast Airlines in September 1958, marking the world's first revenue Friendship service. The type was an ideal candidate in the growing local-service-carrier arena, but West Coast continued to operate DC-3s in smaller markets until the carrier became part of Air West in 1968.

Bonanza Air Lines began transitioning to turboprop service on March 25, 1959, when its first three F-27A Silver Darts began revenue flying. Barely 19 months later, the carrier retired its last DC-3 and claimed credit as America's first all-jet-powered airline, growing the fleet to 16 airplanes.

Long, slim engine nacelles mounted on short, stubby wings was the design hallmark for Lockheed's Electra, an airplane that was larger than the Vickers Viscounts but smaller than the Bristol Britannia. Introduced in 1959, Electras soon brought "jet-powered" airline service to smaller regional cities throughout the world. (Lockheed via Mike Machat Collection)

Close behind, San Francisco–based Pacific Air Lines began flying F-27As up and down the West Coast on May 1, eventually operating an even dozen of the turboprops. The airline began further expansion with

Bonanza Air Lines laid claim to the "first all-jet-powered airline in America" when its last DC-3s were replaced by Fairchild F-27As. The transition took place between March 1959 and October 1960. (Jon Proctor)

The place where the Electra was born passes by the windows as this Eastern Electra takes to the air from Runway 17 at Burbank Airport. The section of the large hangar with the doors closed is the site of the famed super-secret Lockheed Skunk Works. The very beginnings of what became the SR-71 Blackbird program would have been going on inside that building when this photo was taken. (Lockheed via Mike Machat Collection)

Legendary Lockheed test pilot Herman "Fish" Salmon (wearing the orange flightsuit) and other Lockheed personnel discuss a just-completed test flight with the Allison Engine Division Electra at Burbank in July 1958. (Lockheed via Mike Machat Collection)

second-hand Martin 404s about the same time. Together, the two variants permitted phase-out of Pacific's DC-3s, which soldiered on until 1964.

In the eastern United States, Piedmont Airlines began upgrading with F-27s on November 14, 1958, growing its new turboprop fleet to eight. As with Pacific, Piedmont acquired used Martin 404s as well. Seventeen were purchased from TWA to replace DC-3s and came on board three years after the Fairchilds.

The first of seven F-27s for Midwestern operator Ozark Air Lines rolled off the Hagerstown, Maryland, factory assembly line July 16, 1959, and was delivered only 11 days later. But the type did not begin earning revenue for Ozark until the following January. The carrier also flew seven Convair 240s in the early 1960s, then Martin 404s. Like most of the local-service carriers, Ozark continued to operate DC-3s well after the turboprops arrived and finally withdrew them for good in October 1968.

In Alaska, Northern Consolidated Airlines (NCA) and Wien Alaska F-27s transported freight and hearty passengers to small towns in the Last Frontier. NCA took advantage of the F-27B's large cargo door to accommodate bulkier freight, while Wien operated F-27As. In Hawaii, Aloha Airlines operated the original model between Honolulu and island destinations.

Allegheny also operated F-27s but did not receive the type until the end of 1965. By then, carriers were looking to the stretched FH-227 model.

While the F-27 was ideally suited for local-service-carrier routes, the Lockheed 188 Electra became the turboprop of choice for trunk carriers, designed for short- to medium-haul segments while jets were assigned to longer legs. The Electra comfortably seated around 68 customers in four-abreast, first-class layouts plus a spacious, six-seat aft lounge.

On January 12, 1959, the first of 40 Electras began revenue service in the colors of Eastern Air Lines. These all-first-class Golden Falcon turboprops initially seated 66 and operated the carrier's principal routes on the East Coast, spreading their wings to points as far west as San Antonio. It would be a full year before the type was superseded by Douglas DC-8-21s and began concentrating on shorter routes.

American Airlines Electra Flagships would have beaten Eastern's into service were it not for a 22-day pilot strike that began on December 19, 1958. American considered placing the type into service on transcontinental nonstops for a short time while awaiting its first 707s, but the strike scotched that plan and revenue Electra flights began on January 23, 1959, between New York and Chicago, just two days ahead of the first 707 service. Seating capacity was 68, ideal for high-frequency service between Chicago and the East Coast, replacing DC-6 and DC-7 Flagships. The type was only sched-

uled as far west as El Paso. American bought 35 Electras, with an eye toward 25 more, but instead chose additional Boeing jets.

National Airlines, the first carrier to order Electras, took 14 from the factory and later 3 from American Airlines. Configured with 54 first-class and 18 coach seats, the turboprops entered service on April 23, 1959, on the New York–to–Miami route. They became National's workhorse across the route system until the arrival of the airline's first DC-8s in 1960, even serving on longer flights to the West Coast when the routes were awarded to National in 1961.

Dallas-based Braniff International Airways purchased 10 Electras, placing its first into service on June 15, 1959, and the type quickly began appearing at most of the airline's North American destinations. Although sold as first-class service, the 188s featured a 70-seat, alternating four- and five-abreast, arrangement.

Advertised as "a totally new dimension in jet-age travel," Western Airlines began Electra/JET service on August 1, 1959, between the West Coast cities of Los Angeles, San Francisco, Portland, and Seattle. Two months later turboprop flights were added to Salt Lake City, Denver, and Minneapolis, as the fleet expanded to five, 66-seat, first-class-configured airplanes. Seven more Electras followed with the last delivered in 96-seat, all-coach layouts, lacking a lounge. With pure-jet service beginning a year later, the turboprops assumed shorter segments and continued to replace Convair 240s and DC-6Bs.

Northwest was the only U.S. carrier to operate nonstop, coast-to-coast Electra flights, briefly between Seattle and New York, again while awaiting pure jets. Foregoing the aft lounge, the airline's 188Cs were delivered in a mixed configuration featuring both Imperial first-class and Coronation coach. The first was delivered on July 19, 1959, and entered service on September 1, 1959. Medium-haul work was the norm for these 18 turboprops, which were reassigned to even shorter routes with the delivery of more jets.

Intrastate California operator Pacific Southwest Airlines, more commonly known as PSA, found the Electra to be a perfect fit for its routes between San Diego and San Francisco, with most flights stopping at Los Angeles International or Hollywood-Burbank, where the type was built. Seating 98 passengers, including 6 in the lounge, PSA's Electra Jets boasted a 25-minute time between San Diego and the L.A. basin, and one hour to San Francisco. With cheap fares and frequent service, PSA thrived with this rugged airplane, its first type to be purchased new. Initially, three 188Cs replaced four DC-4s, followed by three more Electras including the prototype, refurbished after taking part in the type's certification program.

WELCOME ABOARD THE ELECTRA

Sporting an updated livery, PSA Electra N172PS boards passengers on a sunny morning at Los Angeles during a typical 10-minute stopover. Expedited boarding utilized both the forward and aft doors. (Jon Proctor)

By Jon Proctor

Most first-time travelers aboard the Electra were, like the airlines, transitioning from aircraft such as the DC-6 and Constellation plus, to an extent, Convair and Martin twins. With the Electra's self-contained boarding stairs forward of the wing, one had a chance to get up close and personal with the airplane before even stepping aboard. Compared to the older piston-powered airliners, the Electra looked big, in part because it sat higher off the ground. Its larger passenger windows and fatter fuselage were noticeable, but what really impressed me upon stepping toward the air stairs were the engines and absolutely huge propellers, which reeked of power even while resting at the gate.

Stepping into the airplane, I was impressed with the softer, indirect lighting and a cabin design that gave it a roomy appearance. Soft background music added to the contrast between old and new. Designed for short- to medium-haul routes, most Electras featured carry-on luggage compartments near the forward door. It was almost like boarding a Convair-Liner, yet as I looked aft, the rear lounge mimicked a DC-6 or DC-7, as did the galley adjacent to the second door behind the wings, where I was used to boarding a Douglas.

My first Electra flight was on Pacific Southwest Airlines (PSA), from San Diego to Los Angeles in December 1959, only two months after the type entered service along the California coast. Even in its 98-seat, all-coach layout, it felt roomy, probably enhanced by the six-seat lounge one would not expect to see when riding on a $5.45 ticket.

I chose to sit in the last row of the forward cabin, just ahead of the prop line, so I could see those mighty Allisons fire up. From my window seat, I watched as the props blended into what looked like two giant saucers. Expecting a higher noise level as we pulled away from the gate, I was surprised to feel the brakes release and no increase in propeller rotation, only a slight engine-pitch adjustment. Welcome to the world of constant-speed propellers.

After a short taxi to Runway 27, and no pause to run up engines, the propeller pitch changed again and I was pushed back into my seat as the Electra accelerated rapidly. Unlike the longer takeoff roll I was used to, this bird literally jumped into the air and climbed through the marine cloud layer at a steep angle, bursting into bright sunlight.

PSA kept the cockpit door open in flight (those were the days!), with a red cloth rope across the opening, giving passengers a peek at the front office. Although the flight engineer's seat partially blocked the view, one could see the wide work area that required separate throttle quadrants for the captain and co-pilot.

Although this first flight was smooth, I later found that the Electra's relatively stiff, stubby wings made it more susceptible to turbulence. Its cabin noise level close to the engines was higher, much like the propliners it replaced, but even attached to the propeller, the turboprop engines featured much lower vibration levels, adding to overall passenger comfort.

My PSA flight touched down at Los Angeles International barely 20 minutes after liftoff from San Diego. A propeller-pitch change brought the Electra to a quick stop on the runway, followed by a short taxi to the terminal on Avion Drive. The use of both doors allowed a less-than-10-minute turnaround, yet another Electra feature that made it attractive to airlines, and an ideal fit for PSA.

Here is another example of a prop-era color scheme being applied to a new jetliner still years away from rolling out through the factory doors. Eastern's classic "meatball" scheme, as it was popularly referred to, is applied to a DC-8 in this artist's rendering, and doesn't look all that bad. The large underwing lettering might not have been very effective when the jet was cruising at 35,000 feet. (Mike Machat Collection)

Factory brochure prepared for customer airlines by Boeing details the technical aspects of the new 707, although the jet's final color scheme had not yet been defined. Here we see a DC-7-style paint job as it would have looked on the 707, but American's first airplane was still several years away from reality when this booklet was prepared. It is interesting to note that American was the only U.S. airline to have the engine nacelles painted to match the fuselage markings. (Craig Kodera Collection)

Another clean and classic Raymond Loewy color scheme was developed for application to United's new Douglas DC-8s and Boeing 720s. Nicely complementing American's bare-metal-with-orange-striping motif and TWA's striking red arrowhead design, the red, white, and blue of United's new look was worn on its vast fleet of jets all the way into the mid-1970s. (Mike Machat Collection)

Impending Introduction of the Jets

Even though the first turboprops were entering service and using existing airports without any major problems, airline and airport planners wisely realized that the next generation of pure-jet airliners would require a host of new and improved airport features to safely and effectively accommodate their operations. In addition to the obvious need for longer runways and safety overrun areas, the larger jetliners would require more ramp space for turning and parking, plus wider taxiways and runways to keep their outboard nacelles from hanging out over adjacent grass areas full of potentially engine-damaging debris.

Nicely showing the evolution and progress in airport terminal design is this series of photographs depicting terminals at Los Angeles and New York International Airports. Passengers gather at the ticket counter at LAX in 1952. (Craig Kodera Collection)

Several years later, the terminals did not look all that different as this American Airlines Captain checks in at the ticket counter in February 1961. Type for flight information board in background was set by hand, one letter at a time! (Craig Kodera Collection)

Overhead view of LAX in November 1959 shows the very beginning of the integration process as the new jets entered airline fleets. Note the position of the 707 parked at the end of one of the terminal fingers, away from the gaggle of propliners lined up at the original airport concourses. A United DC-8 can be seen parked under a maintenance hangar overhang at lower left. (Craig Kodera Collection)

Newly designed airport infrastructure was also planned with novel features such as blast fences to keep ramp vehicles from being blown over by jet exhaust. Fully enclosed moveable "jet bridges" designed to shield passengers from the weather would be attached directly to terminal buildings, completely eliminating the need for passengers to be exposed to the elements. After all, it was rather hard to sell luxurious jet service when passengers were being drenched while walking from the gate across a rain-soaked red carpet and up slippery metal boarding stairs to the airplane.

In anticipation of serving both the aircraft and passengers of the Jet Age, airline terminals themselves moved upscale. Large two- and even three-story complexes with floor-to-ceiling dark-tinted plate glass windows and arched or cantilevered roof structures were designed to replace simpler terminal buildings with their cinder-block walls, chain-link fences, and Quonset-hut extensions. In most cases, this new modern look was referred to by the marketing forces of the day as being the "Airport of Tomorrow" to foster even more excitement at the thought of futuristic air travel by jet.

American Airlines' new terminal facade at New York's Idlewild Airport was the largest single-frame mosaic ever constructed when it was finished in 1960. This structure, along with other independently constructed terminals for Eastern, United, Pan Am, and TWA comprised the "terminal city" concept at Idlewild. The terminal also featured separate upper and lower entrance roadways for departures and arrivals, respectively. (Mike Machat Collection)

Inside the new terminal, a roomy grand concourse housed ticket counters and flight information, putting passenger boarding gates within an easy walk at either end. Aircraft nosed into the gates and were connected to the building by short enclosed jet bridges that kept passengers warm and dry at all times. (Mike Machat Collection)

"THE TERMINAL OF TOMORROW"

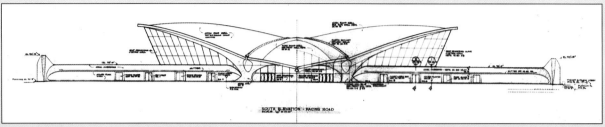

Modern Finnish architect Eero Saarinen created what is considered to be his masterpiece with this ground-breaking design for a terminal building that seemed to fly right off the ground. Located at New York's Idlewild Airport as the crown jewel of its Terminal City loop, the concrete TWA "bird" terminal is seen here in front and rear elevation. (Jon Proctor Collection)

By Mike Machat

As a young airliner enthusiast growing up on Long Island during the 1950s, a trip to New York International Airport (then called Idlewild, and now JFK) was even better than going to Disneyland because *real* jet airliners were making their proud debut here by the end of that decade, turning the airport into a virtual fantasyland of its own. A new, ultimate "Airport of the Future" was being built to accommodate the needs of air travel in the burgeoning Jet Age, and the revolutionary concept of each major airline having its very own distinctive terminal building was utilized in the creation of "terminal city," a two-mile circle of individual buildings creating a veritable skyline of airport architecture.

Located on either end of Idlewild's new International Arrivals Building (IAB) on the airport's southern flank were the brand-new terminals of both U.S. international flag carriers, with Pan American World Airways' open-air umbrella-style building on the west side, and Trans World Airlines' swooping "concrete bird" terminal on the east. These strategic locations allowed both airlines to disembark international passengers at the IAB for U.S. Customs processing, and then after towing the aircraft over to their respective terminals next door, they would service the aircraft and board passengers for new departing flights.

TWA's magnificent terminal was designed by the renowned Finnish architect Eero Saarinen as a "living sculpture" to look like a giant bird poised for takeoff. Days after its official opening ceremonies on May 28, 1962, I visited the airport as a young teenager, full of anticipation at seeing what was, at that time, probably the world's most futuristic and revolutionary piece of industrial architecture. I stood there, staring up in awe at the brand-new building—a bit more diminutive in size than I'd originally expected, but visually stunning, none the less, in all its gleaming white concrete and deeply tinted glass.

Walking inside that terminal for the first time was like entering a space station. Vast expanses of white hand-laid miniature circular tiles complemented by fire-engine-red upholstered furnishings led to large, airy waiting areas, curving ticket counters, posh restaurants, and a space-age information desk with flight information displayed in a pod seemingly hovering overhead. Most intriguing to me, however, was the tubular entryway to the satellite gate area. In the pre-security age of the early 1960s I simply strolled out to see the airplanes through this softly lit, Muzak-filled, red-carpeted passageway that looked as if it could have very possibly led to a waiting Martian spaceship.

I gazed longingly at the upstairs Lisbon Lounge Bar where such legendary personalities as Frank Sinatra and Ava Gardner sat waiting to board their flights to exotic locales all over TWA's route system. Pope Pius IV was also there during his October 1965 visit to New York, and one can only imagine the colorful stories of celebrities, movie stars, show-business legends, and heads of state, all of whom traveled through this terminal when it was new. And as if all this wasn't futuristic enough, New York Airways Sikorsky S-61 helicopters shuttled TWA passengers from this terminal to yet another bustling fantasyland—the New York World's Fair in 1964 and 1965.

In retrospect, the future turned out a bit differently than we'd expected back then. Those atom-powered supersonic flying cars and helicopter jetpacks never quite materialized, but gave way instead to personal computers, cell phones, BlackBerry Smartphones, and GPS. More amazingly, TWA's first 707-131s carried only 111 passengers, yet were flown by a crew of four. They were powered by four turbojet engines that sported a voracious appetite for JP-4, and were deafening to boot. By comparison, the last Boeing 757 to depart this terminal in 2001 flew on two turbofan powerplants that each produced more than twice the 707 engine's thrust. That airplane carried 178 passengers flown by two pilots, and was far more quiet, fuel-efficient, and ecologically friendly than anything ever dreamed of during the 707's inaugural era.

With air travel being such an entirely different experience today, we will simply have to remember the glory days of DynaFan-powered StarStream 707s pulling up to the jetways, with passengers dining in the Paris Cafe and celebrities having one last drink at the Lisbon Lounge before jetting off to Europe, Africa, or the Far East. Now, as an integral part of JetBlue's stunning new JFK terminal, the former TWA "Terminal of Tomorrow" still stands silently in solemn tribute to the dawning of the Jet Age.

Photo of actual TWA terminal building showing the graceful bird-like shape seemingly touching down for a landing. Although no longer used as an active passenger terminal today, the pioneering structure is still there, now preserved as a historical landmark. (Jon Proctor Collection)

Larger ramp areas with a variety of different gate configurations were being built for the first time, and the grand interiors of these new terminals bore more than a casual resemblance to the large spacious shopping malls also making their first appearance in America. Depending on the size of the airport, these impressive new structures either housed many airlines collectively, or individual carriers by themselves in a cluster of separate new buildings. These grand assemblages were linked together by sweeping circular roadways, and were envisioned as being great new "terminal cities."

The aforementioned blast fences were more than just a convenience, as jet exhaust waves would prove to be a formidable hazard for unprotected vehicles and personnel in close proximity. Also, before enclosed and elevated jet bridges protected people boarding or deplaning jetliners, unsuspecting passengers could be blown over or lose their carry-on luggage crossing an unprotected ramp while walking out to board their jet.

By the mid-1950s, airport studies performed in conjunction with aircraft manufacturers were conducted to measure and extrapolate data for new jetliner flight- and ground-operation manuals. These studies revealed the need to cope with surprisingly strong amounts of jet exhaust blast. For instance, the four turbojets of a parked Boeing 707 spooled up to 80-percent power to move the aircraft off its tires' flat spots and begin forward turning motion on the ramp would produce an

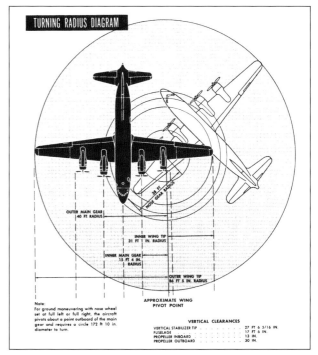

Manufacturer's operating manual shows the turning radius and ramp clearances necessary for safe ground operations with the Douglas DC-4/C-54 aircraft. Clearances for wingtips, tail, and propeller discs were critical in avoiding potentially dangerous situations for both the aircraft and ground crew. (Courtesy of John K. Lewis via Mike Machat Collection)

exhaust velocity of nearly 30 mph at a distance of more than 100 feet behind the airplane.

Exhaust temperature was another dangerous factor, with heat of as much as 700 degrees F emanating from the engine exhaust aperture, diminishing to 150 degrees F at the tail of the airplane. Jet exhaust velocity at full takeoff power was measured at a formidable 1,000 feet per second at the exhaust cone of the engine nacelle. At that velocity, unprotected cars driving on a perimeter road behind a jet

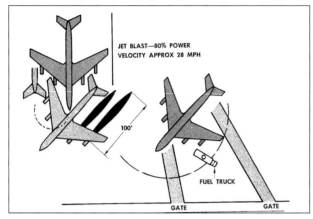

Chart from the Boeing 707 operating manual shows an added element of danger with the jet's exhaust blast being a factor in turning clearances. It is evident that the concept of enclosed jet bridges for passenger loading and unloading had not been thought of when this artwork was created in 1956. (Mike Machat Collection)

at full takeoff thrust would be blown over like a child's toy. The front of the jet engine also posed a potentially fatal hazard to ramp personnel with overpowering suction from the air intake replacing spinning propeller blades as the number-one ground safety threat.

Fueling the new jetliners would also be a different experience for ground handlers. The days of placing ladders against wing leading edges, then climbing up and walking out on top of the wing while trailing a fuel hose and nozzle would soon be ending. The first big advance for fueling the big jets was underwing fueling capability, meaning that two men, each operating a 6,000-gallon F-6 fuel tanker truck, could hook up underwing hoses and fuel the entire airplane in one continuous operation. This was a welcome change for ground crewmen having to walk around on top of the wings, opening fuel-tank caps and then filling one tank at a time on a Constellation or DC-7.

Further advances would eliminate the fuel truck altogether, as underground pipes fed fuel stored in large airport fuel-tank "farms" to valves and hose hook-ups located in the ramp itself just below the parked airplane's wings. This way, ramp fueling personnel could plug hoses from these outlets into small mobile pumping units and then connect those directly to the underwing attach points of the jetliners, thus reducing the amount of large vehicles needed to service the airliner.

Speaking of vehicles, new types of ground equipment would also supplement, and in some cases eliminate

Graphically demonstrating the transition period from props to jets, we see a TWA Boeing 707 at Chicago-O'Hare surrounded by a sea of ground equipment as listed on page 99. Manually pushed boarding stairs exposed to the elements soon gave way to fully enclosed and extendable jet bridges attached directly to the terminal building. (Jon Proctor)

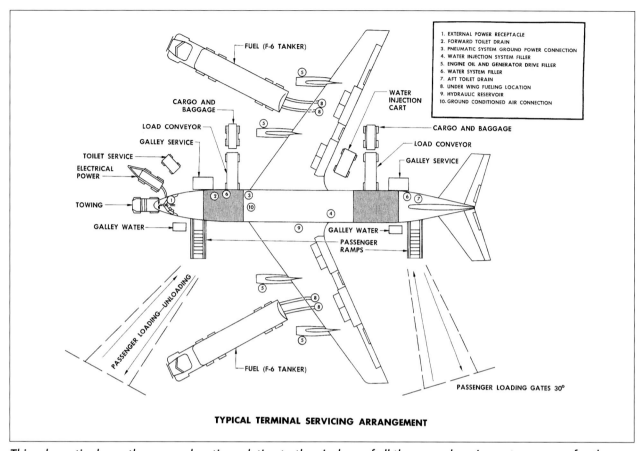

1. EXTERNAL POWER RECEPTACLE
2. FORWARD TOILET DRAIN
3. PNEUMATIC SYSTEM GROUND POWER CONNECTION
4. WATER INJECTION SYSTEM FILLER
5. ENGINE OIL AND GENERATOR DRIVE FILLER
6. WATER SYSTEM FILLER
7. AFT TOILET DRAIN
8. UNDER WING FUELING LOCATION
9. HYDRAULIC RESERVOIR
10. GROUND CONDITIONED AIR CONNECTION

TYPICAL TERMINAL SERVICING ARRANGEMENT

This schematic shows the proper location relative to the airplane of all the ground equipment necessary for the new 707. Compare this layout to the photograph (on page 98) of an actual TWA 707 being serviced at O'Hare Airport in Chicago. (Mike Machat Collection)

altogether, standard prop-era ramp vehicles such as electrical power carts, lavatory trucks, and baggage-handling tugs. Engine-water trucks would be required to pump aboard the alcohol and distilled water mix for water-injected takeoffs. Galley delivery trucks the size of small moving vans would back up to the airplane, their aft sections rising to the height of the cabin floor, to deliver meals and other galley provisions directly into the cabin. Large galley loading doors designed into the airframe would define how differently the new jets would be operated from all the other airliners that had come before.

These new galley doors were located fore and aft on the right-hand side of the airplane at main cabin floor height. Also on the right-hand side but below the cabin floor were large forward and aft baggage doors that allowed baggage and freight to be loaded aboard conveyer belts angled up to the open baggage bay. Ground power connections were also located on the right side of the jetliner's nose to facilitate ramp personnel operating safely away from passengers loading on the left side of the airplane.

As originally intended before the jets entered service, each airplane would be surrounded by an armada

of ground vehicles upon arrival at the gate and while being turned around for its next flight. A typical fleet of ground vehicles and service apparatus required for handling the new jets parked at a terminal was expected to include:

- External power cart
- Forward lavatory service truck
- Aft lavatory service truck
- Forward baggage bay cargo and baggage conveyer truck
- Aft baggage bay cargo and baggage conveyer truck
- Engine-oil and generator-drive filler service
- Ground tug for towing or pushing on the ramp
- Potable-water service truck
- Right wing F-6 tanker truck
- Left wing F-6 tanker truck
- Forward door passenger-loading ramp truck
- Aft door passenger-loading ramp truck
- Ground air-conditioning truck
- Water-injection service truck
- Truck for engine "air-starts"

A large part of aviation's popularity in the 1950s was due to the convenience offered for even inner-city travel. Los Angeles Airways began 10-passenger Sikorsky S-55 helicopter service from Los Angeles International Airport (LAX) on November 22, 1954. Having replaced the smaller Sikorsky S-51 carrying mail and passengers around the vast L.A. basin, the S-55s proved to be a boon to local commuting and were later upgraded to turbine-powered 28-passenger Sikorsky S-61s in 1962. (Los Angeles World Airports)

The East Coast counterpart of L.A. Airways was New York Airways (NYA), linking that metropolis' three major airports with downtown Manhattan. Commuter service was provided using twin-rotor 15-passenger Vertol 44s. NYA also upgraded to jet-powered helicopters in the early-1960s using 25-passenger Boeing-Vertol 107s. Note flotation gear mounted on the big Vertol's landing struts to ensure passenger safety when flying over the open waterways of New York City. (Mike Machat Collection)

The de Havilland Comet 4's massive flaps gave it slower approach and landing speeds. This more powerful and stretched version of the original Comet 1 resurrected the proud de Havilland name after suspension of Comet service following a rash of fatal accidents from 1952 to 1954. (Allan Van Wickler Collection)

By the mid-1950s, airport management staffs and their in-house planners and designers had begun to look at the special needs of the new breed of jet-powered airliners. At this stage, however, the very first seedlings of these new ideas were just beginning to sprout. As we will see, by the time the new jets actually entered commercial service several years later, more refined and effective advancements would be incorporated into airline operations and modern airport design.

Aircraft of the Era

The Jet Age had begun. The world's newest and best jet-powered airliners, both turboprop and turbojet, were now entering commercial service. Lockheed had America's only propjet, while big four-engine jetliners from industry giants Boeing and Douglas were grabbing all the headlines. Britain's improved Comet 4 was making up for the Comet 1 saga, and a rugged twin-turboprop from the Netherlands brought jet service to regional carriers.

Lockheed 188 Electra

The enigmatic Electra was offered to the airlines in two basic versions: 188A and 188C. The first and most popular model had a gross weight of 113,000 pounds and was the model of choice for the majority of domestic U.S. carriers. Engines were the Allison 501D-13 or -13A. The C-model airplane had a characteristically Lockheed increased gross weight of 116,000 pounds, a strategy remembered so well from the Constellation series of aircraft. Engine choice for this airframe was the 501D-15 with its 300-shp (shaft horsepower) increase in power.

Unlike on the BOAC Stratocruisers and DC-7Cs that preceded it, the Comet 4's interior was virtually noise and vibration free. According to BOAC ad copy in 1958, the Comet 4 offered passengers a "fusion of speed and rock-like stability [yielding] an impression of being suspended comfortably in space." Interior configuration shown here featured 16 first-class sleeper-seats in the forward cabin and 43 tourist seats aft. (Craig Kodera Collection)

This extra power was used to lift an additional 1,100 gallons of fuel, which boosted the range of the Electra beyond its originally planned 2,500 miles, all the way to 3,460. The B designation was an unofficial tag used internally by Lockheed to denote the Electra with navigator stations and extra lavatories destined for use by the international airlines.

Passenger capacity for the Electra was normally 66 to 80, with a high-density version available to seat 98. Maximum speed clocked-in at 448 mph at 12,000 feet while normal cruise was listed as 373 mph. Two propeller choices were available also, with the Aeroproducts being the most common and recognizable on the Electra, or the Hamilton Standard design, which was easily identified by its bowed-out shape and rounded tips (these were the propellers chosen for the P-3 series of aircraft for the U.S. Navy). KLM chose the Ham-Standards, as did Capital Airlines, although the Capital aircraft were never actually delivered to the airline, because it had been absorbed into United Air Lines.

A combined total of 170 aircraft were built, the last of which was delivered to Garuda of Indonesia on January 15, 1961. Electras remained in airline service worldwide through the 1980s, and served as freighters for yet another decade, proving the longevity, profitability, and ultimate success of America's only four-engine turboprop airliner.

de Havilland Comet 4

When de Havilland's original Comet 1 fell victim to the edict that "being first is sometimes not being best"

after a series of design-related accidents occurring shortly after it entered service in 1952, the commercial Jet Age found itself temporarily on hold. Canada's Avro Jetliner was also unable to deliver the goods at that time (see Chapter 1 sidebar, "Avro Jetliner: The Other First Jet," page 17), but a subsequent redesign of the DH-106 airframe resulted in a new, improved, and much safer aircraft with even better performance than its progenitor.

First and foremost was the new airplane's modified fuselage construction and ovaloid-shaped windows to forever avoid the ravages of pressurization-induced metal fatigue that plagued the original design. Then, with 10,000-pound-thrust Rolls-Royce Avon 502 engines replacing the original airplane's 5,000-pound-thrust Ghost turbojets, a totally new Comet was born. Along with a higher gross weight of 162,000 pounds and fuselage lengthened to 112 feet, the Comet 3 prototype more closely resembled the larger 78-passenger version of the original design initially ordered by Pan American. Further refinements such as the addition of two "slipper" auxiliary fuel tanks mounted on the wing outboard leading edges created the production Comet 4 series, which became the first truly intercontinental version of the proud British aircraft.

With a launch order for 19 Comet 4s placed in March 1955, BOAC marched steadily toward regaining the jet airliner crown, knowing full well that new competition from the recently announced Boeing 707 and Douglas DC-8 Jetliners in the United States was looming. As we now know, it was a BOAC Comet 4 that indeed beat the United States to the punch by inaugurating commercial jetliner service across the North Atlantic on October 4, 1958, two weeks before the first Pan Am 707 carried passengers on that route. With further uprated Rolls-Royce 524 engines, the Comet 4 possessed a range of 3,225 miles and found a host of new international airline customers in the process.

Further variants of the now-successful design included a lighter-weight, 101-passenger short-haul version called the Comet 4B, operated initially on inter-European routes by BEA. The "ultimate" Comet was the 4C model, with a further-stretched 118-foot fuselage length and 2,590-mile range. Comet 4s were flown by such diverse airlines as Mexicana, Aerolineas Argentinas, East African

Rising from the ashes of the ill-fated Comet 1, the Comet 4 beat Boeing's 707 into transatlantic service by two weeks, flying for BOAC between London and New York. (BAE Systems)

Pan American's glory years during the Jet Age all began with this airplane, the Boeing 707-121. Appropriately named Clipper America *(as were several of Pan Am's first 707s during their initial proving flights and promotional tours), this first jet signaled the beginning of a new age in transportation. As advanced and futuristic as these airplanes were in 1958, it was rather amazing that only two years later they were made obsolete by larger, longer-range, turbofan-powered successors.* (Ren Wicks/Mike Machat Collection)

Airways, Malaysian, Kuwait, and Olympic, but the title of world's final Comet operator went to charter carrier Dan-Air which had the distinction of being the only airline to fly all three models of the Comet 4 series.

Although the Comet's last commercial passenger flight took place on November 9, 1980, the Nimrod, a larger maritime patrol version of the Comet 4 developed for the Royal Air Force, was still flying until the turn of the century. Having first entered military service in 1969, these formidable aircraft were continually upgraded and modified, with the final versions being built by British Aerospace. Larger "next-generation" Nimrods, equipped with uprated turbofan engines and the latest in military electronic wizardry, first flew in the 1990s and are still in operation today. While these newer patrol jets are decidedly more advanced airplanes than the original Comet 4, it is a proud testimony to the ruggedness and adaptability of the Comet design to see descendants of an aircraft type first flown in 1948 still in operation more than six decades later!

Boeing 707-100/200/300/400

Boeing's original 707 variant, the -120, was ordered by American carriers for its ability to operate nonstop on any segment within the continental United States. In addition, Pan American Airways' managers were willing to use the domestic version on transatlantic routes, with fuel stops, in order to gain a competitive advantage. The type could be shifted to shorter routes, such as to Latin America, upon delivery of longer-range 707-320 Intercontinentals. Pan Am became the first operator of the 707 in revenue service, on October 28, 1958, between New York and Paris via Gander, Newfoundland.

With a maximum takeoff weight of 247,000 pounds, four Pratt & Whitney JT3C-6 engines, each producing 12,500 pounds of thrust, powered the -120. Augmented by distilled water injected into the powerplants, total thrust was boosted to 52,000 pounds. The type was marketed with a 121-seat capacity in an all-first-class, five-abreast layout, or up to 179 seats in a high-density configuration. Its maximum range, with a full payload, was 3,075 miles. Utilizing a 13,500-gallon fuel capacity, the airplane could cross the country with relative ease.

When it was decided to offer both first-class and coach service on the jets, a planned five-abreast premium layout was abandoned in favor of four across in the forward, quieter premium cabin, with six-abreast in the aft coach section. But the mix contained a much higher percentage of first-class seats than we see today; in fact, American Airlines split the capacity evenly, with 56 seats in each cabin.

American attained the distinction of operating the first pure-jet flights "across the United States" on January 25, 1959, with its 707 Jet Flagships, nonstop between New York and Los Angeles. But it was partially upstaged when Pan Am leased one of its new 707s to National Airlines for a daily round-trip between New York and Miami, starting on December 10, 1958. Although flown in Pan Am colors, the 707 provided National with bragging rights as first to fly domestic jets in the United States, and was particularly pleasing to the airline's colorful president, Ted Baker, who enjoyed upstaging Eastern's legendary Eddie Rickenbacker at every opportunity.

TWA began New York to San Francisco service on March 20, 1959, with just one 707-120 while principal

Unlike Pan American, TWA held off overseas jet service until its intercontinental 707-300s arrived, eliminating the need for fuel stops on flights to Europe. An example is seen at New York–Idlewild's International Arrivals Building (IAB), wearing the twin-globe logo scheme adopted two years after entering service. (Jon Proctor)

stockholder Howard Hughes struggled to finance the balance of a 15-airplane order. Continental Airlines introduced its Golden Jet 707-120 flights on June 8, 1959, between Los Angeles and Chicago. Western Air Lines, with two 707-120s originally ordered by Cubana and leased from Boeing, began service June 1, 1960, on West Coast routes between Los Angeles, San Francisco, Portland, and Seattle. The pair was acquired as an interim measure while awaiting delivery of Boeing 720s.

Braniff Airways ordered basic 707-120 airframes with larger, JT4A-3 engines that brought about the 707-220 variant and provided improved takeoff performance at the airline's high-altitude destinations, and gave it a speed advantage. Braniff advertisements boasted the "fastest flights" when beginning jet service on December 19, 1959, in the Dallas–to–New York market against archrival American Airlines.

The first non-U.S. carrier to order and operate Boeing jets was Australia's Qantas, which opted for the basic 707-120 with a shortened fuselage to extend its range for longer segments across the Pacific. The unique "short-body" 707-138 was not added to the 707-120

WELCOME ABOARD THE 707

By Jon Proctor

As with the Lockheed Electra, early 707 operations utilized boarding steps rather than jetways—those covered bridges that are today's norm. Using this conventional form of embarking on one's first jet flight, unless the weather was bad, provided an exciting preview. You could not help but be awestruck by the sheer size of this new behemoth.

The use of separate aircraft doors for first-class and coach passengers was a short-lived phenomenon, done away with when space constraints dictated nose-in parking and single-point boarding. Status-minded customers soon learned that you could board through the first-class entryway by waiting until the last minute because the aft coach door was closed first, in order to facilitate engine start-up.

As a teenager, my only thought was to board my first jet flight as soon as possible, on a TWA 707, from Chicago to Los Angeles in September 1959. Thanks to the generosity of my brother, I had the extra $7 to purchase a "jet surcharge" coupon necessary to upgrade from a Super-G Constellation flight, and was eager to find a good seat. On early jet flights, coach seat assignments were not available on "through" trips, and TWA Flight 29 had originated in Pittsburgh.

Perhaps it was my imagination, but the air conditioning seemed better on this jet than on an older DC-7, as the cool air hit my face as soon as I entered the airplane. Walking forward toward seat 18A, I immediately noticed the PSUs, or passenger service units, that hung from the open, overhead racks. Each unit contained a "Fasten Seat Belt" and "No Smoking" sign,

Passengers board an American Airlines Boeing 707 Flagship New Jersey at Los Angeles International in the transitional days before fully enclosed jet bridges attached directly to new satellite terminal buildings to keep passengers protected from the elements. (Craig Kodera Collection)

three air vents, individual reading lights, and a small speaker to pipe boarding music through the cabin. There was plenty of legroom on this airplane, even in coach. Each row enjoyed two of the smaller windows, and the seats were deep and comfortable.

Instead of plug-in tray tables, each seatback included a drop-down tray. The traditional propliner window curtains were replaced by window shades that could be pulled up or down. Side lighting came from a panel that ran the length of the cabin on either side, just above the windows. In the ceiling above the aisle were circular fixtures that seemed to serve no purpose on this daylight flight. Later, I learned that these "domes" contained lighting that could be adjusted from "bright" to "night," and were designed to replicate portholes in the aircraft ceiling. The night setting featured pinholes of light against a dark background, giving the impression of a planetarium filled with stars.

The air conditioning produced a constant hum as boarding was completed. Together with the airplane's soundproofing it was sufficient to mask any engine noise, and I suddenly became aware that the airplane was moving, backward. It was my first time experiencing pushback from a gate with a tug attached to the nose gear. The first hint of engine noise came as we taxied away from the gate to the runway.

The 707 seemed to taxi as a stable platform, rather than the subtle bouncing I remembered from piston-powered airliners; it moved rock-solid as we taxied along. Although there was no prop-era engine run-up, the Boeing was eased onto the runway, aligned for takeoff, and then stopped. Now the engine noise level rose to a rumble, gaining power. Finally, the brakes were released and we slowly lumbered down the runway, gradually increasing speed. After what seemed like an eternity, the front of the cabin rose and our jet broke ground with a bit of a thump as the main landing gear rotated before retracting into the fuselage. The engine noise subsided a bit, no longer bouncing off the tarmac, as the ground fell away.

"Yankee Pot Roast," served for lunch, was the first truly hot meal I could remember on an airplane, with an accompanying beverage in a real glass. There were no carts in the aisles to block access to the three aft lavatories that featured flush toilets, another first.

The aft cabin noise level could not truly be described as quiet but in marked contrast to a propliner it was all but vibration free. Less than four hours later, TWA Flight 29 landed at Los Angeles International Airport, more than two hours sooner than I would have arrived on the Super-G Constellation on which I had originally booked space. But the thrill of an early jet came at a price. I never did get to fly on a Super-G.

This work by famed artist Ren Wicks depicts the dome lighting of TWA's 707s, designed to look like portholes in the aircraft ceiling. At night, pinholes of light against a dark background gave the impression of a night sky filled with a galaxy of stars. (TWA/Jon Proctor Collection)

The unique 707-200 series, built at the request of Braniff International, combined the Model 100 fuselage with more-powerful JT4A-3 engines used by the -300 model. Only five examples were built, including one that was lost in a pre-delivery demonstration and acceptance flight accident. (Boeing/Jon Proctor Collection)

The first 707-138 for Qantas sits on the ramp at Boeing's Renton plant shortly after rollout. Boeing engineers removed 10 feet from the 707-120 fuselage design, aft of the wing, to bring about the "short-body" 707-138; Qantas was the only customer. In the background new 707 jets for TWA, American, and Continental receive finishing touches before their first flights. (Qantas)

certificate, nor did it attract additional customers. Qantas placed the type into service on July 29, 1959, on the multi-stop route between Sydney and San Francisco.

Boeing's intercontinental 707-320 was first delivered to launch customer Pan Am in July 1959, and was specifically engineered for transoceanic flights with increased passenger and cargo capacity. Its fuselage was stretched 8 feet 5 inches, bringing the maximum passenger load to 189. A 21,200-gallon boost in fuel capacity came from a center fuselage tank and additional tankage in the wings, increasing the -320's range to 4,360 miles.

The -320 wing also featured an enlarge planform with a 12-foot increase in span, a new leading-edge airfoil at the wing root, and increased area of the inboard trailing-edge flaps as well. The same JT4A-3 engine assigned to the 707-200 powered the intercontinental version, and a total of 69 were built for Air France, Pan Am, Sabena, and TWA.

An otherwise carbon copy of the -320, the 707-420, was equipped with Rolls-Royce Conway 50B bypass engines. A total of 37 were sold to eight overseas carriers, the first being, quite appropriately, BOAC.

One of United's first Douglas DC-8 jet Mainliners, N8002U was upgraded from Model-11 to Model-21 standards. It still wears delivery colors in this March 1968 photo at New York-JFK, differentiated only by the emergency and door exit outlines legislated into existence by the FAA in 1965. (Harry Sievers)

Dramatic ant's-eye view of a factory-fresh Eastern Air Lines Douglas DC-8-21 taxiing out for takeoff at Long Beach, California, on a pre-delivery acceptance test flight. This Raymond Loewy color scheme was the third of nine different variations on the same design theme to be applied to Eastern aircraft within a two-year period, but was perhaps the epitome of the original design. Compare the tail's Falcon motif with that of the Eastern DC-8 on page 113. (Mike Machat/Craig Kodera Collection)

The DC-8's cockpit was much roomier and offered much greater outward visibility than that of its piston-powered predecessors. Flight Engineer's station is visible to the right with an observer's jump seat at extreme left. Note moveable sunshades mounted on a circular track to ensure placement anywhere they were needed, a unique Douglas feature. Emergency quick-donning oxygen masks seen hanging next to each seat were a new addition for the flight crew. (Mike Machat Collection)

Douglas DC-8-10/20/30/40

Trailing the 707's entry into service by nearly a year, the first Douglas DC-8 was delivered to launch customer United Air Lines on June 3, 1959. Powered by the same Pratt & Whitney JT3C-6 engines mounted on Boeing's 707-120, the DC-8-10 featured a heavier, 265,000-pound maximum takeoff weight and a substantially greater range of up to 3,900 miles. At just over 146 feet in length, it was 2 feet longer than the 707-120, with a maximum density listed at 176 passengers.

Delta Air Lines accepted its first DC-8-10 on July 21 and wasted no time showing it off to the public; a day later it set a 1-hour 21-minute speed record between Miami and Atlanta. A second DC-8 was accepted on September 14.

Both carriers began DC-8 revenue flights on September 18, 1959, with Delta beating United into actual service entry by virtue of their time zones. Its Flight 823 departed for Atlanta from New York–Idlewild at 9:20 AM Eastern time, while United's Flight 800 left San Francisco at 8:30 AM for New York, but in the Pacific time zone.

Unlike Boeing's overwater version of the 707, Douglas' DC-8 Intercontinental was the identical size as its domestic brethren, offering only a higher gross weight allowing for more fuel carriage, and uprated Pratt & Whitney JT4A turbojets. The Panagra example seen here was used by that carrier for service between the United States and various South American destinations. (Mike Machat Collection)

WELCOME ABOARD THE DC-8

By Craig Kodera

What an exciting time to be flying commercially: 1960. The Boeing 707 has made its debut and is now plying the airways, having beaten the Douglas DC-8 into service by a year. But the -8 was something special, and as the Douglas sales folks were saying, well worth the wait.

Until then, Douglas had been the undisputed leader in commercial airline transport aircraft, while Boeing built bombers. Douglas may not have been first, but the company learned from others' mistakes and refined the jetliner concept. What emerged was a beautiful engineering accomplishment, which was designed to make both passengers and airline bosses happy.

When approaching the DC-8, a passenger cannot help but notice the height of the airplane, especially since it sat up on its main landing gear with a nose-down attitude. One could readily see this because the world was still utilizing external boarding stairs on a ramp outside a terminal. This only served to increase the juxtaposition of flight experiences between the props and the jets.

One other attention grabber was the "translating rings/ejectors" or reverser rings for each engine, designed to slide back on rails in the lower pylon while the airplane was in a landing configuration. Interestingly, this feature accomplished two other actions: noise suppression and inflight drag inducement much like using spoilers to help increase descent rate without increasing airspeed.

Upon entering the cabin, a Douglas design feature immediately presents itself in the form of a forward lounge, placed in a dedicated space ahead of the main cabin. Much like the DC-6B and DC-7, the forward lounge had its own distinctive pair of windows. Decor was late-1950s chic, with vinyl upholstery and "space-age" colors and shapes in the furnishings. How delightful it will be to visit this area during our flight.

Arriving in our first-class cabin, we notice the unique Douglas-designed Palomar seats. These seats were state of the art at the time, and had in their headrests all of the passenger service unit amenities, rather than mounting them overhead. It was just one more way the DC-8 engineers tried to pamper Jet Age passengers.

But by far the most wonderful aspect of flying in a DC-8 was its windows. Those wonderful, expansive

Passengers board a United Douglas DC-8-21 in this carefully staged publicity photo taken at Long Beach Airport in 1958. In the foreground is a baggage tug with carts of individual baggage containers that held luggage and small cargo and were hoisted up into the under-floor baggage bays forward and aft of the wing. This novel Douglas feature became the standard method of baggage loading many years later as wide-body transports made their debut. Note the carpet, and stewardess positioned atop the boarding stairs ready to welcome everyone onboard. (Craig Kodera Collection)

Jet flight in the Stratosphere at 600 mph was as futuristic as it got in 1960, and this view from the window of a Pan Am DC-8 shows you why. (Allan Van Wickler)

windows were the largest on any jetliner. Thankfully this design feature was held over from DC-6 and -7 days, and we are sure to have a wonderful sightseeing trip in the DC-8 as a result.

Once underway, the airplane has the feeling of being rock-solid. The movement is hardly noticeable. Then the sound of the JT3 engines comes alive as they begin spooling-up for takeoff, the soft turbine whine settling into a low rumble. We're off and on our way on Douglas-firm wings. You never have to worry about the structural integrity of a Douglas airliner.

Having enjoyed all the passenger comfort items we had found on a DC-8, we realize our time in the air is almost at an end. As the flight draws to a close we notice that during our descent the DC-8 is a very "slick" aircraft design, one that can easily overrun an airport without careful planning by the cockpit crew. And here come those reversers now! On the ground with a solid touchdown, we can thank Douglas for another fine airplane. The Jet Age is certainly here, and the ride is wonderful.

A United DC-8 passenger gazes out the picture window located at each row in that aircraft, showing the passenger amenities housed in each of the aircraft's seats. Note window curtains at either side of the portal, a vestige left from the days of the propliners that soon gave way to lighter, simpler integral sliding window shades. This seat placement, a long-standing Douglas innovation, soon became obsolete when the need to change seat pitch based on travel seasons and peak travel times created row positions located between the windows themselves. Later Douglas jetliners did away with this window configuration. (Compare window size and placement on the Boeing 707 shown on page 104.) (Mike Machat Collection)

Only Delta and United purchased DC-8-10s, with a total of 28 being built. Within four years, both carriers had begun upgrading them to turbofan-powered DC-8-50s.

In much the same way as Boeing hatched the 707-200 series, Douglas created its DC-8-20 by upgrading the -10 airframe with the more powerful Pratt & Whitney JT4A turbojets planned for the long-range DC-8-30. This resulted in an airplane tailored for operations into hot and high-altitude airports, with an increased maximum takeoff weight of 276,000 pounds. Aeronaves de Mexico, Eastern, National, and United bought a total of 34 airframes. In addition, United upgraded 15 DC-8-10s to the Series 20 standard.

The first factory-delivered example was accepted by Eastern Air Lines on January 3, 1960, and entered service on January 20, advertised as the DC-8B, a designation once marketed by the manufacturer and what seemed like a natural follow-on to Eastern's DC-7B Golden Falcon service. Following a complaint to the CAB by Delta, however, Eastern was ordered to drop the "B" designation for the DC-8.

National Airlines initiated DC-8-20 service on February 11 between New York and Miami, technically becoming the first airline to simultaneously operate

both the 707 and DC-8 by virtue of its 707 leasing agreement with Pan Am.

For long-haul operations the basic DC-8 airframe was equipped with uprated JT4A-9, 16,800-pound-thrust engines, and fuel capacity was increased from 17,500 gallons to 23,400 gallons, creating the DC-8-30 series. Pan Am's Chairman Juan Trippe, who insisted on having the more robust powerplant to gain the international range his airline's routes required, ordered it first. The JT4A was a civil version of Pratt & Whitney's new J75 turbojet being used in several of the Air Force's new supersonic Century Series fighters at the time.

Unlike the long-range 707-320, the DC-8's fuselage was not stretched, nor was its wing area enlarged, but maximum takeoff weight was increased to between 300,000 and 315,000 pounds depending on the variant (-31/-32/-33). These changes increased its range to 4,700 miles, resulting in transatlantic capability, even to southern European destinations. Fifty-seven DC-8-30s were sold to 10 airlines including U.S. carriers Northwest and Pan American, which was first to put the type into service on March 27, 1960, between New York and Bermuda, and then later to Europe and South America.

The DC-8-40 variants (-41/-42/-43) were identical to the respective DC-8-30 series, but powered by

17,500-pound thrust Rolls-Royce Conway R.Co.12 bypass engines. Thirty-two were delivered to Alitalia, Canadian Pacific, and Trans-Canada Airlines. TCA accepted the first Series -40 on February 4, 1960, and began service on April 1 between Toronto and London via Montreal.

Fokker F.27

While trunk carriers grew quickly with higher-capacity airliners, local-service carriers suffered from a lack of rapid traffic growth, which produced a need for more efficient aircraft replacements with a smaller increase in passenger payload. Convair-Liners and Martins provided the required number of additional seats but were more expensive to operate than the DC-3s, with only a marginal increase in speed.

Dutch manufacturer Fokker began developing a DC-3 replacement in 1950, after abandoning the concept with the advent of World War II. The resurrected design called for 32 seats, later increased to 40. The first F.27 Friendship took to the air on November 24, 1955, from Amsterdam's Schiphol Airport.

Not surprisingly, managers of 11 of the 13 local-service carriers inspected the new design in Holland and were favorably impressed. Four carriers—Bonanza, Frontier, Piedmont, and West Coast—placed orders for the F.27 in 1956, to be manufactured under license in the United States by Fairchild Aircraft Corporation. Although Frontier later canceled its order, Allegheny, Ozark, and Pacific went on to fly the turboprop airliner.

Purchase of new equipment, a first for local-service carriers, was assured by financing from the U.S. government's Aircraft Loan Guarantee Act, signed into law in September 1957.

The rugged, high-wing twin utilized Rolls-Royce Dart 511 (R.Da.6) turboprop engines that had been proven in use on the pioneering Vickers Viscount. Its U.S.-built variant (designated F-27) first lifted off from Hagerstown, Maryland, on April 12, 1958. It was certified three months later and began carrying revenue passengers with West Coast Airlines on September 28, nearly two months ahead of the first Fokker variant, which was placed into service by Aer Lingus. With a cruising speed of just over 320 mph, the airplane was nearly twice as fast as the DC-3 it replaced and represented the first turbine-powered U.S-built airliner to enter commercial service. The F-27 also introduced local-service passengers to the comfort of built-in air conditioning.

More-powerful Dart R.Da.7 engines resulted in the F-27A model, followed by the F-27B with a larger cargo door. Later variants, the F-27J and F-27M, offered even greater engine power. Like the DC-3s it replaced, the Friendship was nearly self-sufficient on the ground with steps built into the passenger door on the Fairchild aircraft, and waist-high cargo-door access.

The success of this remarkable turboprop airliner would eventually lead to a stretched version. The F.27 Mk 500 and FH-227 followed in the mid-1960s pushing the type's production run to an impressive total of 786, including 205 Fairchild-built airplanes.

Banking away over the winding Mississippi River in an artist rendering, this Ozark Fairchild F-27 carries its 40 passengers to destinations throughout the Midwest. Built under license from Fokker in the Netherlands, the Fairchild turboprop first entered revenue service in September 1958, and set the standard for twin-engined turboprop transports for many years to come. (Mike Machat)

WELCOME ABOARD THE FAIRCHILD F-27

By Craig Kodera

From the moment you entered the new airplane, you were impressed with its self-contained air conditioning and smart, modern interior. Perhaps the biggest revolution in the cabin was the use of *very* large elliptical windows; installed to take advantage of the captivating aerial views this high-wing airplane afforded its passengers. Every seat was a good seat for enjoying these inflight vistas. One of the thrills about flying in the F-27 was the ability to watch the tall main landing gear retract and extend right outside your window.

In all the years of airliner history, truly, there was nothing similar to the Rolls-Royce Dart engine. It had a screech, a warble, that filled one's entire body with a humming sensation unlike anything ever experienced in piston-engined aviation. From the ever-increasing whine during start-up, to the instantaneous application of takeoff power, the consistent, smooth pull of the Dart was more like driving one of today's electric cars versus one run by pistons. The airplane didn't pound its way into the air, but rather seemingly rode on a rail. Once airborne, flying in the Fairchild had a different "seat-of-the-pants" feel to it. Hanging from a wing rather than riding on top of the wing made for a unique and improved passenger experience. It always felt somehow smoother in that airplane.

In the Hawaiian Islands, Aloha Airlines began replacing its DC-3s with Fairchild F-27s in 1959. (Allan Van Wickler)

Chapter Eight

COAST-TO-COAST IN ONLY FIVE HOURS
(1959-1961)

Golden Falcon Jet, *an Eastern Air Lines Douglas DC-8-21 in 1960.* (Mike Machat)

The Boeing 707, Douglas DC-8, and Convair 880 enter commercial service by the end of the 1950s, and the traveling public begins to experience the wonderment and excitement of jet flight for the very first time. Speeds and altitudes that were once highly coveted world records set by high-performance experimental military aircraft are now the domain of traveling businessmen and families going on vacation. The Jet Age has arrived.

The Commercial Jet Age Begins

As Boeing began delivering its 707 jetliners to the airlines, the type began route-proving flights to the first cities scheduled to receive jet service. These operations were designed to familiarize not only flight crews but ground staff as well. Pan American Airways, which had the distinction of being the first carrier to have its livery appear on a 707, accepted the initial airplane on September 29, 1958, and began training flights carrying cargo and mail between New York and San Juan under the type's provisional airworthiness certificate.

Noise restrictions at Idlewild Airport limited initial flights to daylight hours and limited the type's maximum takeoff weight to 190,000 pounds, well below its 247,000-pound capacity. Similar restrictions were imposed at London's Heathrow Airport and noise regulations forced Pan Am to initially use Le Bourget Airport at Paris rather than the preferred Orly.

Even as Pan Am managers were preparing for jet service, they began discussing a lease arrangement with National Airlines that would allow National to operate Pan Am's 707s on a turnaround arrangement between New York and Florida during the winter months, with Pan Am gaining the right to lease future National DC-8s for transatlantic flights. With word of a possible stock exchange as part of the deal came rumors that it would be the first step in an eventual merger of the two airliners. Such speculation, as it turned out, was premature.

Although Pan Am became the first 707 operator, it was briefly upstaged by BOAC and its smaller de Havilland Comet 4s, which began operating between London and New York–Idlewild on October 4, 1958, a scant two weeks ahead of its U.S. competitor. As we learned earlier, neither the Comet 4 nor the 707-120 had reliable nonstop transatlantic range, but even with fuel stops, they shrank the travel time sufficiently to justify replacement of piston-engine nonstop service. Several months passed before larger 707-320s began crossing the Atlantic uninterrupted.

Over at American Airlines, managers were so eager to begin turbine-powered flights on long-haul segments that they contemplated interim transcontinental flights utilizing turboprop Lockheed 188 Electras until 707s could begin flying the routes. However, the plan was negated by a pilot strike that delayed service entry by both types, which then made their debuts within only three days of each other in January 1959.

Jet service was gradually added by other carriers as 707s continued to roll off the production line at Renton, Washington. Douglas DC-8s began serving the airlines in September 1959. By the end of December, the Jet Age was in full swing, with 75 pure-jet airliners in service, along with an even greater number of turboprop aircraft. Even factoring in the cost of new equipment, the jets could produce more airline revenue by completing four trips in the same time it took propliners to complete three, while easily enjoying double the passenger and cargo capacity.

Aircraft floodgates opened at manufacturers Boeing, Douglas, Fairchild, and Lockheed in order to more than triple the population of turbine fleets worldwide. Air travel was about to expand tremendously.

The Learning Curve

With every major step forward in aviation comes a learning curve in the form of incidents and accidents from which new aircraft design features and operational procedures emerge to prevent recurrences. It is an unfortunate but inevitable step in the advancement of progress during which valuable machinery and precious lives are lost, but life-saving improvements in safety and performance are the valuable results of this process. Perhaps only in retrospect can we understand just how safe and reliable today's modern airliners have become. Unlike in the early 1960s, it is now a rarity to have a news bulletin suddenly interrupt a radio or TV program blaring out that there was another major airliner crash with the loss of all onboard.

Complete with all the associated pomp and circumstance, Pan American's first Boeing 707 service from New York to Paris prepares to receive its passengers at Idlewild on a rainy autumn night, October 26, 1958. Although a BOAC Comet 4 snuck under the wire two weeks earlier to beat the 707 to the punch inaugurating the world's first transatlantic jet service, Pan Am still relished the moment as the first U.S. carrier to provide that capability. (Mike Machat Collection)

From Props to Jets

Saturday, October 4, 1958, saw the world's first two jet airliners together for the very first time at New York International Airport. On the observation deck of the International Arrivals Building a crowd of nearly a thousand spectators greeted the BOAC Comet that had just flown the world's first commercial revenue passenger service across the Atlantic in a jet transport. Not to be outdone, Pan Am's Juan Trippe ordered one of his new 707s, in New York that day on a route-proving flight, to be parked at the adjoining gate when the Comet arrived from London. The 707 simply dwarfed the smaller British jet, its fuselage polished to a mirror finish. Excitement filled the air along with the new scent of kerosene, and the piercing jet-engine noise was simply deafening. No one in attendance really cared, however, for this was the moment that signaled the official start of the Jet Age. (Sykes Machat photos)

As the first new jets entered service in 1958 and 1959, they were flown by seasoned airline veterans considered by their companies to be the "best of the best" in terms of piloting skill and ability to command a $5 million aircraft with up to 150 souls on board. New onboard systems, powerplant management, flight characteristics, and operating procedures had to be learned, and emergency procedures were practiced incessantly, committed to memory, and then mastered in the air. With this new breed of airliners, jet-age training and methodology was required to bring its veteran prop-era pilots up to speed. Classroom training could only go so far, however, and because full-motion simulators had not yet come into the ground training fleet, real aircraft were taken off the line and used for flight crew assimilation and pilot checkouts.

February 3, 1959, was a particularly black day in aviation history. On that cold winter evening, American Airlines' first Lockheed Electra—an airplane in service for only 10 days—crashed into the upper East River while on approach to New York's LaGuardia Airport. In Clear Lake, Iowa, that night, a chartered Beechcraft Bonanza crashed on takeoff killing rock-and-roll legend Buddy Holly and fellow rockers Ritchie Valens and "The Big Bopper." Midway over the North Atlantic on a routine passenger flight from Paris to New York that same evening, a Pan American Boeing 707-120 experienced autopilot failure while flying at cruise altitude, causing commercial aviation's first recorded "jet upset" where the airplane unexpectedly departed straight-and-level flight and plunged 29,000 feet toward the ocean.

Miraculously, the crew of the Boeing 707-120 was able to wrestle the controls and pull out of the nearly inverted dive a scant 6,000 feet above the waves, thankfully saving all onboard including famed American dance legend, Gene Kelly. In testimony to the big Boeing's rugged construction, the airplane held together through the ordeal, but suffered minor structural damage as a result of heavy g-loads induced during the recovery. And speaking of recovery, only three weeks later, another Pan Am 707 shed an entire engine and pylon during a minimum-control airspeed demonstration while on a training flight from Le Bourget Field in Paris. The crew managed to regain control and land at London's Heathrow Airport where Pan Am had better maintenance facilities than at Paris.

The learning curve also applied to the news media and how they dealt with Jet Age emergencies. In July that same year, another Pan American 707 lost two wheels from its left main landing gear while taking off from New York and, after burning off enough fuel, returned to Idlewild Airport to make a successful emergency landing on a foamed runway. Unbeknown to airport authorities, however, news of the impend-

ing emergency was being broadcast "live" via local TV and radio stations. By the time the crippled jet landed, a crowd of more than 50,000 curious onlookers had invaded the airport grounds in order to see the expected crash. They stood literally by the side of the runway, much to the chagrin of rescue crews trying to reach the jetliner!

In August, the first fatal training accident of the Jet Age occurred when an American Airlines 707-120 rolled inverted at low altitude and crashed into a field after executing a two-engine-out missed approach to Calverton Airport on eastern Long Island. The practice crew of three pilots and two flight engineers were killed. Similar training accidents claimed a Braniff 707 later that same year, a Delta Convair 880 in 1960, a TWA 880 and another American 707 in 1961, and a Western Airlines Boeing 720B in 1963. These tragic losses made a compelling case for the development of more-sophisticated cockpit simulators to replace inflight training whenever possible.

By the end of 1962, operational turbine-powered airliners that crashed while in passenger service included a United DC-8 in Brooklyn (midair collision), an Eastern Electra in Boston (bird ingestion on takeoff), a Braniff Electra in flight over Texas (wing separation), an Aeronaves de Mexico DC-8 in New York (runway overrun), a Northwest Electra in flight over Indiana (wing separation), a United DC-8 in Denver (emergency landing), an American 707 at New York (rudder malfunction on takeoff), a Sabena 707 on landing at Brussels, Belgium, an Alitalia DC-8 landing in Bombay, India, a Varig 707 landing in Lima, Peru, and two Air France 707s—one on approach to Paris and the other landing in bad weather at Guadeloupe, West Indies.

When examined in historical perspective, these 18 accidents exacted an exceedingly high toll in terms of human life and machinery lost. However, because they occurred at the beginning of the learning curve, significant knowledge was amassed and equally significant improvements were made in aircraft design, operating procedures, and even air-traffic control. For instance, leading-edge slats and other high-lift devices were added to the Boeing 707, allowing lower landing speeds and better maneuverability. Ventral fins were also added to the 707 to allow greater inherent stability at low speeds and high angles of attack during landing. To reduce the risk of midair collisions, aircraft speeds were reduced to a 250-mph maximum below 10,000 feet.

As other lessons were learned from subsequent accidents and incidents over the years, continual improvements in airframe and powerplant design, onboard systems technology, and operational procedures were made that eventually led to the impressive safety record we enjoy for all types of commercial airliners today.

Overall Impact of Jet Airliners on World Travel and Commerce

Turbine-powered airliners made a huge impact on world economics almost from the day they entered revenue service. Now imagine doubling capacity while simultaneously halving travel times and lowering costs. Such were the rewards when modern jets and turboprops began replacing piston-powered aircraft, some of which had been flying since the end of World War II.

Across the Atlantic, a mind-numbing 10 to 12 hours of reciprocal engine noise and vibration were replaced by less than 7 hours aboard an airplane that burned cheaper kerosene and actually allowed conversations inside the cabin without raising one's voice. Flights were smooth enough for delighted passengers to marvel as they built playing card "houses" or balanced quarters on drop-down tray tables.

The timing could not have been better, with growing economic prosperity on both sides of the Atlantic ready to welcome increased capacity and at lower fares. Even during the first nine months of 1959, with limited jet service, traffic was up 13 percent, while capacity rose only 5 percent. Aboard the jets, Economy class quickly replaced Tourist class, while 20 percent of customers were still flying in First class. Pan Am's jets achieved an 86-percent load factor, which was unheard of until that time. Within a year, passenger loads on its jets jumped from 55 percent of available capacity to 80 percent.

The advent of jet travel also ended the domination of steamship travel between the United States and Europe. While some of the great ocean liners soldiered

American Airlines' Chairman C. R. Smith made the cover of TIME *magazine in recognition of his efforts to launch transcontinental jet airliner service, thus cutting travel time in half. This is symbolically represented in this masterful portrait by artist Boris Artzybasheff with the depiction of a watch literally being sliced in half by the jet exhaust at upper left.* (Craig Kodera Collection)

New DC-8s line the West Ramp at Douglas Aircraft Company's Long Beach plant in this photo taken on December 30, 1959. Aircraft being delivered to Delta, United, and Pan American are prepared for their shakedown flights before entering passenger service, and the tail of DC-8 prototype Ship One can be spotted third from the end. The DC-8 production line remained active until May 1972 when the 556th transport was delivered to long-time Douglas customer SAS. (Mike Machat Collection)

on for several years, their blue-ribbon speed records were eclipsed by the formidable combination of jet comfort and lower ticket prices. With the available speed of the jet airliner, passengers began traveling to and from Europe for long weekends, something they would have never considered after making a five-day crossing of the North Atlantic by ship, or even a 12-hour airplane ride aboard a Constellation or DC-7.

Even more amazing is what the new jets, and even turboprops, did for business travel. Prior to jet service, trips across the country and back, at minimum, required three days. Now a round trip could be completed in less than two days, with the "road warrior" arriving at business meetings fresh and alert, then returning home much the same way. Airfreight was delivered expeditiously as well, diverting perishables such as fruits and vegetables to spacious jet cargo holds.

Along with passengers, aircrews completed their work more quickly, enabling much improved utilization of pilots and flight attendants. Aircraft builders employed more workers to keep up with heavy produc-

tion as airline managers all but begged for faster delivery of new airplanes. Even engine manufacturers shared in the bountiful revenues, along with the various parts manufacturers and other airline-related businesses.

Aircraft of the Era

With first-generation jetliners now routinely flying the world's commercial routes, a new advanced breed of aircraft made their debut. Neatly filling the niche between four-engine and twin-engine jet transports was a new mid-size entry from Convair and a modified and slightly smaller airplane from Boeing. Not to be outdone, an advanced turboprop from Great Britain and an improved twin-jet from France brought regional turbine-powered airline service to the world.

Boeing 720 and Convair 880

Even before the ink was dry on purchase contracts for the first American-built jetliners, airline managers were thinking ahead to their need for medium-haul route capacity that would not require as many seats as the 707 and DC-8. Most U.S. carriers placed orders for turboprops aimed at short-haul routes, leaving a gap in between.

Flush with the success of its short-haul line of airliners, San Diego–based Convair was a likely candidate to enter the same market with turboprops or jets. Its popular Convair-Liners were rolling off the Lindbergh Field assembly line at a rapid pace in 1953, but company managers already had their sights set on a successor aircraft. Approached by billionaire Howard Hughes, they briefly considered building a civil version of the YB-60 military jet bomber, then still in the design stage. Hughes wanted the airplanes for Trans World Airlines, in which he held controlling stock, but the proposal was not pursued.

Over the next few years, Hughes and the manufacturer held meetings that eventually resulted in a contract for 30 Model 22 Skylark 600 Jetliners. The four-engine design was to carry 80 passengers on

The Convair 880's sleek lines and elegant proportions are apparent in this pre-delivery photograph. TWA operated a total of 28, including one briefly leased from Northeast Airlines, making it the largest Convair jetliner operator. (Convair/Jon Proctor Collection)

With its trademark Golden Falcon emblem adorning the tail, an Eastern 720 approaches its assigned gate at West Palm Beach, Florida. The airline opted for more powerful JT3C-12 turbojet engines. Four over-wing emergency exits, instead of the standard two, were provided for the option of high-density seating on Caribbean routes. Although not utilized, this feature increased the resale value of Eastern's 720s when they were sold to charter carriers. (Jon Proctor)

Although it never had a firm purchase order in place, Northeast Airlines leased six airplanes from Hughes Tool Company to become the second operator of the type, after Delta. It would fly a total of 10 Convair 880s between December 1960 and January 1968. One is seen here on a snowy evening at Montreal. (Convair/Jon Proctor Collection)

medium-range segments but, at Hughes' insistence, would have transcontinental range. The program was launched on the Hughes order plus a contract with Delta Air Lines for 10 airplanes, bringing the total to 40 Skylarks, the minimum number to proceed required by the board of directors at the General Dynamics Corporation, which by then was Convair's parent company. (The decision to move into a different market arena was based on Convair's argument that a suitable jet engine was not available for smaller, short-range jet designs. This would come back to haunt company executives in years to follow.)

Evolving from its initial design, the Skylark was briefly named Golden Arrow, then simply Convair 880, a number matching its proposed speed in feet per second. And speed was its calling card. To be the "world's fastest jetliner," its graceful aerodynamic lines included a super-thin wing and narrower passenger cabin. Initial plans called for utilizing the same Pratt & Whitney J57 engine planned for the 707 and DC-8, but a switch was made to General Electric's military J79 powerplant that powered the B-58 bomber, once its design was released for civil use.

In Seattle, Washington, the Boeing sales team and engineering department responded quickly. Executives reasoned that Convair's entry could cut into follow-on 707 orders. The solution was a shortened, lighter ver-

sion of its product that would contain a large percentage of interchangeable parts. Called the 707-020, it put a dagger through Convair's heart when United Air Lines, about to sign a substantial order for the 880, instead bought the Boeing model. Ironically, United was not a 707 customer, and its president, W. A. "Pat" Patterson insisted on renaming this new model. The number 720 was agreed upon, in order to reflect an improvement over the 707.

Boeing had shelved an earlier 720 design, the 717, but was able to resurrect the concept by reducing the weight of forged metal parts, using thinner skins and structures, and incorporating a lighter JT3C-7 engine, thus providing an attractive alternative to Convair's 880. However, the biggest factor in its success came with widening the fuselage cross-section to increase Coach seating capacity from five- to six-abreast, matching that of the 707. Its length was 8 feet 4 inches shorter than the 707-120.

Another significant feature of the 720 was a highly efficient wing, with an increased angle of incidence between the fuselage and inboard engines plus full-span, leading-edge flaps that reduced takeoff and landing speeds by up to 11 mph, depending on gross weight. This combination of improvements gave the airplane the advantage of increased performance at airports with shorter runways.

TWA's 880s initially featured a luxurious 12-seat lounge. The layout was in anticipation of an all-first-class cabin but the type instead entered service with a split configuration that included 35 coach seats. (Convair/Jon Proctor Collection)

Convair struggled to bring in additional orders, but only managed to produce 65 880s, including 17 of the heavier 880M (M for "modified") models marketed to foreign carriers. Even with its greater speed, the type's limited capacity clashed with rapid growth in passenger traffic; more seats became the deciding factor.

Boeing 720 sales eventually reached 154, although 89 were turbofan-powered "B" models (see Chapter Nine). But it was considered a successful program because of the minimal research-and-development expense required to spin off the design from the 707, and the type kept airline customers in Boeing's stable and away from competing manufacturers. Further validating the decision to produce a limited-production-run aircraft is the fact that 70 percent of 720 customers went on to purchase hundreds of Boeing's new 727 tri-jets.

Vickers Vanguard

As early as 1953, while the Viscount was being introduced on its routes, BEA started discussing with Vickers the idea of a "Viscount Major" for service entry in 1959. This enlarged airplane was envisioned as a 100-seat aircraft with range out to 1,350 miles. After going through the preliminary processes with the airline, both parties knew immediately that a stretched and enlarged Viscount would not be able to meet BEA's requirements. Enter the Model 870.

At the same time BEA was showing interest in an aircraft larger than its Viscounts, TCA also expressed a desire for an airplane to suit its expansive domestic network. The British airline originally wanted a high-wing aircraft because response by passengers to the Airspeed Ambassador fleet was so positive: Every fare had an unobstructed view to the outside. TCA found exception with this configuration based on its flying environment in Canada, and once all the requirements from both carriers were added into the mix, a double-bubble fuselage cross-section with low-mounted wing became the winning planform.

From early on, the Rolls-Royce Dart was excluded from consideration on the Vanguard (named such by BEA) in favor of the promised new engine from Rolls, the RB.109, later named the Tyne. The standard powerplant developed 4,000 shp, some 50-percent more horsepower than the prototype engine. The production configurations of the Vanguard for each of its two customer airlines were numbered 951 for BEA, and 952 and 953 for TCA. The latter carrier wished to have a higher-gross-weight aircraft to carry more passengers in an all-coach layout, and the Canadian models were another 6,000 pounds heavier than those of BEA.

First flight of the big Vickers took place on January 20, 1959, and the prototype airplane lacked the dorsal

The first Vickers Vanguard 952 for Trans-Canada entered service on February 1, 1961, two years after the type's maiden flight; only 43 were built. (BAE Systems)

fin ahead of the vertical stabilizer that the later production airplanes incorporated. The Vanguard was a big airplane, slightly larger than the Lockheed Electra, and could carry more passengers. It had a hefty new 28-volt DC electric service, which allowed for self-generated starts if no ground equipment was available.

The Vanguard entered scheduled passenger service with TCA on February 1, 1961, although BEA had been supplementing its Christmas schedule with Vanguards two months prior. The final delivery of a 952 to TCA took place on April 3, 1964, and final passenger service in Canada was flown in 1971.

Vickers' Vanguard was a good, stout, and sturdy airplane. After its passenger-service days ended, the Vanguard enjoyed a second life in the air-cargo business; a role originally designed into the airplane all those years prior. In the end, only 43 airframes were produced, and only BEA and TCA were original operators of the airplane. The Vanguard, like the Britannia and the Electra that came before, found itself squeezed between the end of the prop era and the beginning of the new jets, its fate made all the worse, however, because it was the last of the three.

This color photograph shows the beautiful lines of the Caravelle VI-R, enhanced even more in United Air Lines colors. (Jon Proctor Collection)

Caravelle VI-R

By the early 1960s, the term "Cadillac" applied to anything representing the zenith, and the upgraded Caravelle VI-R model was certainly the "Cadillac of Caravelles." Compared to the original Caravelle I and III models (see Chapter Five), the VI-R (pronounced "six-r") represented a quantum leap in development for the world's first rear-engine jetliner, with significant improvements in cockpit ergonomics, passenger comfort, and overall aircraft performance. This was also the ultimate operational configuration with the Caravelle's original 105-foot-long fuselage, until stretched and re-engined versions were produced several years later.

The most visually apparent change from the first Caravelles was the larger side windows and "domed" roofline for the cockpit, greatly enhancing roominess and outward visibility for the flight crew. For certain airlines, the trademark avionics hump above the rear fuselage extending back to the aircraft's dorsal fin was removed with the advent of newer and more efficient communications and navigation systems antennae. Thrust reversers (the "R" in VI-R) were added to each engine nacelle, and power for the aircraft's twin Rolls-Royce Avons was increased from 11,400 to 12,600 pounds of thrust each. Maximum takeoff gross weight was also increased from 101,410 to 110,230 pounds.

Making its first flight from the Sud facility at Toulouse, France, in February 1961, the VI-R was quickly certified for commercial operations in the United States, and the first of 20 aircraft ordered by United Air Lines began revenue passenger service that July. A total of 56 VI-Rs were produced and were the last turbojet-powered Caravelles before larger fanjet versions made their appearance later in the decade.

WELCOME ABOARD THE CARAVELLE

By Mike Machat

For some reason you can tell quite a lot about an airplane just from the way it rides while taxiing on the ground. The loping and almost floating sensation of the great Douglas propliners was decidedly different than the stiffer ground ride of the Constellation with its tall, slim nose gear for instance. But all that gave way to a more "riding-on-rails" sure-footedness when the new jets entered service. Taxiing along in the Sud Caravelle felt like the best of both worlds, as the ground-handling attributes of the low-slung jetliner were enhanced by its rugged four-wheel-bogey main landing gear. The airplane feels well planted on the ground; much the way a wide-track luxury sedan feels at speed on a freeway or autobahn.

With its low wing and ample flap area, the Caravelle's takeoff is nothing less than regal. The airplane's large semi-swept wing has an "iron leading edge" (meaning no lift-enhancing leading-edge flaps or slats), yet the Caravelle handles beautifully at approach speeds and all the way down to the runway. Slotted sailplane-like spoilers also give the pilot precise control for the airplane's rate of descent without appreciably adding to or depleting its airspeed. The

Caravelle was always a favorite with its pilots, from the original "steam-powered" models, as they were affectionately called, to the more advanced version flown by United Air Lines. Passengers benefited from this new jet experience as well, with a significantly quieter cabin, thanks to the aircraft's rear-mounted engines, and of course, those huge triangular-shaped windows placed strategically at every seat row.

Passengers board a Finnair Caravelle on a regional flight from an outlying smaller city to Helsinki, Finland. (Mike Machat)

With the original Caravelle cockpit and nose section having been literally grafted onto the fuselage from Britain's de Havilland Comet, French engineers at Sud-Est realized that a modernization was required as the aircraft became more advanced in the early 1960s. With United's order for the VI-R model, a new enlarged windshield and improved instrument panel layout was designed, and here are the results. Cockpit visibility was nearly doubled, and cockpit ergonomics were enhanced greatly as well. Pilots the world over loved to fly the airplane. (Mike Machat)

UNITED'S MAGNIFICENT CARAVELLE

It happened every Monday through Friday at precisely 5:00 PM at United's new terminals at both Chicago's O'Hare and New York's Idlewild Airport: Marching in single file to board the rear stairs of the sleek French twinjet SE 210 Caravelle VI-R was a conga line of nattily dressed businessmen carrying leather briefcases and wearing gray flannel suits with white button-down shirts and skinny black ties. It was the beginning of the hip 1960s and the dawning Kennedy era of America's greatness, and what better way to show the world what this country was all about than having airline service for men only!

Yes, as unique and politically incorrect as that may seem today, United's famous "Men Only" service was perceived as a special perk for successful businessmen heading off to, or returning home from, important business meetings in a time before women CEOs, astronauts, and race car drivers, as well as video conferencing. In another seemingly astonishing move, cigars were not only permitted on those flights, but were provided to passengers by the stewardesses themselves—the only two women aboard the aircraft. With its four-abreast seating and large triangular windows, the 64-seat jetliner was an instant hit with passengers, and United's New York Executive and Chicago Executive men-only flights

Historic photo of an actual United Caravelle at Idlewild Airport in 1962 awaiting its passenger manifest that will be comprised of "men only." The 5:00 pm departure headed for Chicago, while a similar flight left Chicago at the same time destined for New York, and carrying men only. In tribute to their homeland, the elegant-looking aircraft were named for cities in France, the one pictured here is Ville de Lille. (Mike Machat)

were an instant success with business clientele. United's men-only flights continued until January 1970 when the newly formed National Organization for Women (NOW) took legal action, and filed suit to officially end the service.

Effectively filling the void in aircraft size at the beginning of the commercial Jet Age, the Caravelle offered short- to medium-range service on routes more suited to the aging propliners remaining in operation, as larger four-engined jets began to command the trunk lines. American Airlines, United's chief competitor, maintained Douglas DC-6B and Lockheed Electra turboprop operations to smaller cities on its route map (the new "CVL" code began to appear on United's timetables in the column showing aircraft type). Perfectly suited to stage lengths from 800 to 1,200 miles, United's pure-jet Caravelles soon became a familiar sight in the skies over the eastern half of the United States.

In retrospect, history now regards United's Caravelles with somewhat mixed results after that fleet carried more than 10 million passengers over more than 117 million miles from July 1961 to October 1970. Although passengers favored the diminutive jetliner, the same could not be said for United's maintenance staff, which had to deal with the aircraft's cantankerous Rolls-Royce Avon 532R engines surrounded by an all–Pratt & Whitney–powered fleet. From both an operational and training standpoint, having mixed engine types, cockpit logic, and cabin layouts within the same airline always added complexity and cost, but in the Caravelle's case, the trade-off was that United was able to beat its competition on short- and medium-range routes with pure-jet service until the advent of the Boeing 727 and Douglas DC-9 in the mid-1960s.

United announced its groundbreaking $60 million order for 20 Caravelle VI-Rs in February 1960 as the first foreign-built jet transport ever adopted by a U.S. airline. Ironically, they entered service on July 14, 1961—Bastille Day in France. As so often happens in aviation, history repeated itself; in November 1993 United once again broke ranks and selected the Airbus A320 as its mainstay medium-range jetliner, opening the door to more North American Airbus customers in following years. Once again, an advanced twin-engined jetliner flown by two pilots and built in Toulouse, France, was proudly plying American skies.

Chapter Nine

STAGE TWO: THE FANJETS
(1961-1962)

Clipper Stargazer, *a Pan American Boeing 707-320B in 1962.* (Mike Machat)

As good as the new jetliners were for transporting passengers on worldwide routes at 600 mph, these first-generation aircraft gulped copious amounts of fuel and produced noise levels that were almost painful at close range. A further improvement to the turbine powerplant ensues with the development of the "fanjet" engine, which not only helps solve the fuel and noise issues, but generates even more thrust than before.

Commercial Jetliners Reach Maturity with True Intercontinental Travel

The path to full intercontinental jet travel was paved with many small steps. A dream of airline passengers and airline managers alike, round-the-world passenger jet service indeed originated from humble beginnings. Remember Britain's pioneering Comet 1?

That airplane's first intercontinental route for BOAC in 1952 spanned from London to Johannesburg, connecting northern Europe with Southern Africa. As impressive as that might have seemed at the time, with the Comet's modest 1,500-mile range, the trip had to be made in six legs with stops to refuel along the way. By 1954, BOAC's jet routes extended eastbound all the way to Tokyo, but again that trip had to be flown in 10 segments with the longest single leg from Rome, Italy, to Beirut, Lebanon.

When improved models of the Comet entered airline service in 1958, the airplane's range had been extended to as much as 3,225 miles, allowing BOAC to "steal a march" and beat Pan American to the punch with the world's first transatlantic jet service in October of that year. Still, the airplane had to stop and refuel in Gander, Newfoundland, on westbound flights if winds aloft were less than optimal. Other foreign carriers used several different long-range Comet 4 models to fly on stage lengths as long as Mexico City to Chicago (Mexicana), Bombay to Bangkok (United Arab Airlines), and Paris to Beirut (Kuwait Airways).

With the first Boeing 707-120 and DC-8-30 models, ranges of up to 3,000 and 3,500 statute miles were made possible, respectively. Although a significant improvement over the earlier prototype models they superseded, these gas-guzzling first-generation jets were still restricted to routes where alternate refueling stops were available. Nonstop flights from Europe to the U.S. West Coast or from Tokyo to Honolulu were still only a fantasy in the minds of airline planners everywhere. For now, commercial jet aviation had arrived, and flying aboard a jet airliner was as futuristic as it got, but there was one more step to be taken to advance the art and science of jet-powered commercial air travel to its highest level—the truly intercontinental jetliner.

First to answer that need was Boeing with a new, larger, and more powerful version of its 707 simply called the Intercontinental. Formally known as the 300 series, this new queen of the skies not only made the aforementioned long-range routes possible, but carried higher passenger loads as well. When airline planners factored in the ever-important seat-mile costs (the cost of moving one passenger seat over a distance of one mile), the numbers were quite favorable and airlines

Passenger's-eye view of the forward fan sections of engines three and four on an American Airlines Boeing 720B Astrojet. (Jon Proctor)

were able to pass those cost savings along to their passengers. This factor then drove up demand, and long-range air travel was suddenly becoming more affordable for the casual traveler or family going on vacation.

Boeing 707 Intercontinental service was inaugurated by Pan Am in July 1959, and within one year, many if not most of the world's foreign airlines were introducing either the 707-320 or improved DC-8-30 and -40 series into long-range service. While Pan Am could now fly anywhere on its Pacific routes, rival U.S. flag carrier TWA employed its 707-320 series both domestically and across international routes. European carriers such as Lufthansa employed their Rolls-Royce-powered 707-420 Intercontinentals on routes from Germany to the United States, South America, and the Far East.

These new long-range versions of the first-generation jets proved to be the answer to many international airlines' prayers, but they still operated close to their design limitations as far as engine power and inflight performance were concerned. The longer-range aircraft also consumed copious amounts of fuel as they plied the world's air routes. Would airframe and power-plant technology and innovation result in even better versions of these new airplanes? The answer to that question came only one year later.

"By-Pass" Turbojets and First-Generation Turbofans

The turbofan engine was a significant leap forward in the early jet era. Its design was the logical evolution of conventional jet engines, adding a larger propulsion fan to the basic core to provide substantially greater thrust and greatly reduced fuel burn that in turn allowed more range.

Rather than just settling for the turbine section of an engine powering one set of axial-flow compressors and producing anemic thrust levels, Rolls-Royce engineers added *another* low-pressure compressor section, independent of the first, and ducted the additional air around the core of the engine. This exhaust was routed around the combustion chamber and exited the engine along with the hot core exhaust through the same tailpipe. This helped cool the engine, all the while cooling the jet effluent and lowering the decibel level as well. The by-pass ratio of air in Rolls-Royce's Conway, its first "by-pass" engine, was only a tiny 0.3. The later Spey model increased this to 0.6. It was a win-win compared to a straight turbojet, but obviously not the perfection of a true turbofan.

Rolls-Royce's introduction of the 17,500-pound-thrust Conway as the world's first commercial by-pass engine, spurred Pratt & Whitney to get with the program and take the ratio of their JT3C up to an amazing 1.5. They accomplished this by using a separate fan

Resplendent in its all-white gloss livery, the first Convair 990 poses shortly after rollout from the Convair factory at San Diego. The new jetliner flew for the first time on January 24, 1961. (Convair/Jon Proctor Collection)

Boarding ramp view of the Caravelle 10B's Pratt & Whitney JT3D engine nacelle showing the unique ovaloid air intake shape. These new 18,000-pound-thrust fanjet engines gave the venerable Caravelle a new lease on life, and it soon found success with European charter carriers that used the aircraft to carry revenue passengers well into the 1980s. (Mike Machat)

section on the first compressor. This then became the JT3D, the world's first true operational turbo*fan* jet engine. By-pass turbojets, however, represented a significant bridge, or transition, from the turbojet to the turbofan, and played an integral part in aviation powerplant history.

Not to be left out, General Electric took its 11,200-pound-thrust CJ-805-3B turbojet (civil version of its military J79 engine as used on the Convair 880) and added a separate fan section on the aft end of the hot engine core, using a ducted "flow-through" nacelle that shrouded the entire engine. This proved to be a more aerodynamically streamlined engine structure than having a wider nacelle on the forward fan section only (Boeing 707) or a tapered nacelle with mid-section fan

Among the 707 customers opting for Rolls-Royce Conway engines was BOAC. Seen between flights at New York–Idlewild in June 1962, this aircraft displays the airline's attractive midnight-blue livery. (Jon Proctor)

exhaust (Douglas DC-8). Thus, the 16,100-pound-thrust GE CJ-805-23 turbofan was created, as was tested on the Sud Caravelle, and used operationally on the Convair 990. (Later models of the Caravelle used advanced versions of the Pratt & Whitney JT3D.)

Impact on the Industry from the Turbofan's Advances

Perhaps the most significant added benefit of turbofan engines was the propitious drop in noise levels to

What is a propeller-driven DC-6B doing in this chapter on fanjets? Making the point that some airplanes are almost irreplaceable, Northeast flew its DC-6Bs on shorter intercity routes up and down the Washington–New York–Boston corridor until 1966. Despite the airline having new twinjets and turboprops flying by the late 1960s, nothing could beat the sheer economic advantage of the reliable Douglas propliner on those shorter, commuter stage lengths. (Mike Machat Collection)

the point where cumbersome external noise suppressors were no longer required. With the cooler fan exhaust literally shrouding the hot core section gases as they exited the tailpipe, the painful roar of the engine was mitigated to much more acceptable sound levels around airports, and even when the aircraft were flying over them at higher altitudes. From a purely power standpoint, the fanjet JT3D produced up to 18,000 pounds of thrust compared to the "straight" turbojet JT3C's 12,000 pounds.

Around the country, initial public perception indicated that the first turbojet-powered airliners had earned an unenviable reputation for being much louder than the piston-powered aircraft they replaced. As a result, restrictive rules were imposed requiring sometimes-complex, noise-abatement procedures, particularly on takeoff. The new generation of turbofan-powered jetliners combined the attributes of lower overall-engine-noise levels with improved thrust levels and the ability to climb more steeply on takeoff, thus becoming "good neighbors" wherever they flew.

Aircraft of the Era

The pinnacle of new jet airliners was a series of aircraft possessing intercontinental range, improved aerodynamic features for added safety, and engines that were quieter, more fuel efficient, and more powerful all at the same time. Called "fanjets," these advanced aircraft represented the first significant leap in technology of the burgeoning Jet Age. One of them could land in "zero-zero" weather while another flew at almost the speed of sound!

Even more impressive than a DC-6B still flying in revenue service in 1966 is this Air America DC-4 seen at Misawa, Japan, during summer 1969. This unpressurized workhorse was used to transport U.S. Air Force Security Service personnel and their dependents between various military bases located throughout Japan and the Far East. Although this aircraft had been converted from a C-54G, it was equipped with a relatively luxurious full-passenger interior. (Mike Machat)

Boeing 707-120B/320B

With most Boeing and Douglas jet orders specifying Pratt & Whitney turbojet engines, the powerplant manufacturer accelerated fanjet development and was test-flying its new JT3D model by fall 1960. This extraordinary comeback, combined with the Convair 990's design delays, created a near–dead heat between Pratt & Whitney and General Electric. It also gave Boeing and Douglas the advantage in attracting follow-on orders from existing airlines, whose managers much preferred fleet commonality.

The GE engine's fate was sealed when Pratt & Whitney developed a plan to convert existing JT3C turbojets to 17,000-pound-thrust JT3D turbofans for

The first Boeing 720B for Northwest Airlines is pictured on the flight line at Renton, Washington. After initially ordering Douglas jets, the airline transitioned to Boeing and stayed with the manufacturer until ordering DC-10s some 10 years later. (Boeing/Jon Proctor Collection)

Representing the ultimate in first-generation jetliners is Boeing's Intercontinental 707. This Flying Tiger Line aircraft is a 707-320CF or Convertible Freighter, as identified by the cargo door visible in the forward fuselage. Tiger's 707s, delivered in the mid-1960s, were used for Military Airlift Command charter operations throughout the Pacific region. (Boeing/Jon Proctor Collection)

much less than the cost of straight replacements. American immediately ordered an upgrade to its existing fleet of 707s and 720s, which added 35 mph to the types' speed, and greatly enhanced overall aircraft performance. American also set up a conversion line at its Tulsa, Oklahoma, maintenance base and performed the re-engine work in-house.

Promoted by American as Jet Age: Stage II, the long tradition of calling its airplanes Flagships gave way to a more contemporary name: Astrojet. Its first 707-123B entered service in March 1961 between New York and Los Angeles a full year ahead of the 990's debut. Pan Am also upgraded its 707-120s, and orders poured in for new turbofan-powered Boeings, which then became the standard. Australian carrier Qantas upgraded its 707-138 fleet to turbofans and placed a follow-up order for factory-delivered 707-138Bs.

The 707-320B featured JT3D-3 engines that produced 18,000 pounds of thrust and a range of 6,000 miles, allowing reliable nonstop segments from the U.S. West Coast to European and Asian destinations. Pan Am received the intercontinental fanjet version in April 1962, which was followed closely by the first 707-320C convertible freighter.

Eighty-nine of the 154 720s built by Boeing were produced as turbofan-powered 720Bs, and American also retrofitted its initial 10 airplanes. The type's commonality with the 707 brought follow-on orders from original Boeing jet customers, for the most part at the expense of Convair's 880 and 990.

Douglas DC-8-50 Through -55

Answering the siren song of fanjet power, Douglas showed no hesitation in modifying its DC-8 to utilize the JT3D fanjet engine. This required a new larger-diameter nacelle design incorporating a louver system located in the mid-body casing just aft of the fan section. Douglas engineers fitted 17,000-pound-thrust JT3D-1 turbofans to the prototype DC-8 (N8008D) bringing it up to the DC-8-51 standard and increasing its maximum takeoff weight to 276,000 pounds, identical to the DC-8-21 variant. First flight of that aircraft took place in December 1960, a mere 2½ years after the inaugural flight of the original airframe in May 1958. The "straight-pipe" JT3C turbojets wound up having a relatively short run as the introduction of the Jet Age continued to unfold. Use of the new 18,000-pound-thrust JT3D-3B fanjet powerplant brought about improved performance for the DC-8, ensuring its longevity as a successful first-generation jet transport.

The DC-8-51 was the domestic version with the new fanjet engines, its MGTOW (maximum gross takeoff weight) growing to 276,000 pounds. The -52, -53, and -55 were all intercontinental versions of the series, and their respective gross weights were now 300,000,

Delta Air Lines upgraded all of its early-delivery DC-8s to turbofan engines and Model 51 standards. N820E pulls into its assigned gate at Orlando, Florida, on March 29, 1967. (Jon Proctor)

315,000, and 325,000 pounds, thanks to the new fanjet engines. A key feature of the new turbofan engines was their increased fuel efficiency that allowed the DC-8-55 to carry the same amount of fuel as the earlier non-fan models, but fly farther. Moving the aft bulkhead rearward by modifying the rear galley and lavatory configuration also allowed an increase in total passengers to 189.

KLM, the first European DC-8 operator, gained the distinction of also receiving the first turbofan-powered variant, a Model 53, on April 3, 1961. Showing off its capabilities, the second KLM delivery aircraft flew 6,890 miles nonstop from Long Beach to Rome in 11 hours 17 minutes. The new fanjet-powered DC-8 soon proved to be the most popular of all the standard-body original airframes. So popular, in fact, that it outsold all other versions built up to that time, with 143 being delivered to the airlines. Interestingly, the -50 series also beat the sales of the later stretched DC-8-63, the most ordered of the long 'eights, and except for a few Rolls-Royce Conway-powered DC-8-40s, all subsequent DC-8 deliveries were turbofan aircraft. As with the Boeing 707 and 720, airline managers began ordering retrofits of older models. Delta Air Lines converted its entire DC-8-11 fleet to -51 standards, and United Air Lines upgraded a substantial number of original DC-8s from its fleet as well.

In addition to the all-passenger airplanes, Douglas also sold the series -54CF, -55CF, and -54AF Jet Trader to the airlines. These two CF models were convertible freighters with a large 140-inch-wide cargo door built into the front fuselage so carriers could mix cargo and passengers in the same aircraft. The AF, or All Freighter, was introduced with a 15-aircraft order from United, and this version was designed to carry nothing but freight, being devoid of galleys, cabin windows, or any passenger amenities. The final short-body DC-8 to roll off the Long Beach assembly line was, in fact, a DC-8-54AF.

Convair 990

American Airlines' Chairman C. R. Smith saw the advantage of turbofan power early on, from both an economic and a competitive point of view. In August 1958, he ordered 25 Convair Model 30 jetliners from General Dynamics for $100 million. Commercially marketed as the 600 and later renamed the 990, this follow-on version of the 880 was to be 139 feet 6 inches long with a maximum takeoff weight of 240,000 pounds and powered by General Electric CJ-805-21 "ducted fan" engines to give it a speed advantage over the Boeing and Douglas jetliners already on order. With Pratt & Whitney's turbofan engine development running 18 months behind General Electric, the new Convair jet was only offered with GE powerplants.

A distinctive design feature unique to the 990 was the appearance of four anti-shock bodies mounted on the upper trailing edge of its ultra-thin wing. Resembling large inverted canoes, these pods utilized the same new "area rule" aerodynamic technology that greatly enhanced the performance of supersonic military jets. For the 990, this served to optimize the aircraft's lift/drag ratio at speeds above Mach .80. Additionally, these "speed pods" served as supplemental fuel tanks located optimally close to the airplane's center of gravity.

Convair engineers did a masterful job of evoking the look of speed in their new jetliner. Swept back 39 degrees at the leading edge, the 990's wing planform

This factory-fresh American Airlines Convair 990 shows why the airplane was referred to by pilots as "The Maserati of Jets." American ordered 20 of the sleek jetliners, and flew them until 1968. The domestic version of the airplane as operated by American had a 3,200-mile range and could achieve a maximum cruising speed of 621 mph! (Nick Veronico/Jon Proctor collection)

Registered as N8497H for pre-delivery flight testing, Swissair's first Convair 990 Coronado is seen here flying over undeveloped land east of San Diego, California. The fast jetliner was delivered to Swissair on January 12, 1962, as HB-ICA. (Convair/Jon Proctor Collection)

bespoke superior Jet Age performance, which became a major selling point of the airplane. With the ability to offer 635-mph Blue Streak coast-to-coast nonstop flights 45 minutes faster than the competition, American's managers planned to configure the 990 in an all-first-class layout, with 707s to carry coach passengers on the plebian "slower" flights.

General Electric upgraded the existing CJ-805 design that powered the Convair 880 by adding a fan and turbine on the engine's rear end, saving development time and allowing a higher bypass ratio. By pulling additional air around the basic engine and exhausting it at low velocity through a double-jet nozzle, the production GE CJ-805-23 improved operating efficiency by up to 40 percent over the non-fan model, creating 16,100 pounds of thrust.

Convair executives went ahead with the 990 based solely on American's order, which included a guaranteed 635-mph speed and the ability to operate between New York's LaGuardia and Chicago Midway Airports. It was a particularly bold move, especially considering the attractive purchase contract that included an inflated $22.8 million credit on the trade-in of 25 DC-7s instead of a down payment. Although launch customers normally receive generous discounts, this contract would require a long 990 production run to spread out the costs.

Additional customers proved to be elusive and Convair lost significant orders from Pan Am, Continental, and other customers. In fact, American was the only U.S. buyer, along with a handful of airplanes purchased by Swissair, Varig, and Garuda. Failure to build a prototype aircraft took a heavy toll on General Dynamics when wind tunnel tests failed to disclose significant design problems. Fixing them nearly

resulted in an order cancellation from American Airlines. It was saved by long wait times at Boeing and Douglas and American's need for more jet equipment. Convair granted even deeper discounts on the order and accepted cancellation of five airplanes.

In the end, the modified 990, designated the 990A, could not match its original guarantees and the type entered service with American on March 18, 1962, between New York and Chicago, but using Idlewild and O'Hare Airports; the LaGuardia and Midway plans had been long-since canceled by the type's redesign. Instead of a single, premium-class cabin, 57 coach seats were installed, along with 42 in first class plus a four-place lounge. American's only 990 transcontinental flights operated briefly from San Francisco to New York. Unable to complete the segment against prevailing winds, the 990 flew only the eastbound segment.

Swissair ordered the airplane's overseas version named Coronado, which beat American's 990s into regular service by nine days, and kept its fleet in operation for 12 years. Except for a three-year stint with Middle East Airlines, second-hand 990 fleets served mostly charter outfits and travel clubs for several years but were eventually taken out of service when stiffer noise rules went into effect.

Only 37 990s were built, resulting in massive financial losses. Combined with the 880 shortfall, General Dynamics wrote off $425 million on the program, by far the largest loss of any corporation at the time.

de Havilland/Hawker Siddeley H.S. 121 Trident I

Although not technically a "fanjet," the Trident still deserves mention. Having first flown in January 1962, this novel airliner provides us with a peek into the

British European Airways became the first operator for the Hawker Siddeley Trident with a 24-airplane order. The advanced tri-jet first flew on January 9, 1962. (BAE Systems)

future. It was a smaller airplane than the popular four-engine intercontinental jetliners of the time, and was quite a technologically advanced aircraft as well. Although the Trident may not have been a success when compared to other first-generation jetliners that preceded it, this airplane indeed served as a harbinger of things to come.

The Trident story is fraught with frustration, for had the original 1958 design concept been frozen and heralded into production, such legendary airliners as the Boeing 727 might never have reached production. How can we make such a bold assumption? Simply stated, this aircraft was originally to be a short- to medium-range airliner powered by three Rolls-Royce RB.141 Medway "by-pass" turbojets producing 14,000 pounds of thrust each. The original Trident would have weighed between 130,000 and 150,000 pounds at take-off and carried 110 passengers over routes of up to 1,500 miles in length. (These were the approximate specifications of the Boeing 727, only five years before that aircraft entered service!)

As happens in modern industrialized societies, an insidious combination of politics and corporate wrangling can combine to put a stranglehold on progress, and the Trident succumbed to just this type of industrial "perfect storm." Originating manufacturer de Havilland was caught in the maelstrom of British aerospace consolidation, orchestrating a merger with Fairey and Hunting to form a new company called Airco. Combined with this series of events was the

insistence of launch customer BEA on having the new tri-jet be reduced in size, weight, and capacity to become a 107,000-pound, 80-passenger jetliner. BEA then ordered 24.

This pivotal change was enacted to make the airplane more suitable for the specific needs of BEA at the expense of overall world market appeal, and Britain's airliner industry never recovered from this stumble. Many months of critical timing and market advantage were squandered as design changes were contemplated and then adapted. The Airco merger became moot when de Havilland became a component of the Hawker Siddeley Group. Now powered by three 10,400-pound-thrust Rolls-Royce RB.163 Spey by-pass turbojets, the smaller Trident I finally flew for the first time on January 9, 1962, and slowly reached production and operational status by the end of 1963.

As the world's first airliner to be certified for "zero-zero" autoland operations (precursor to today's full Category III landing capability), the Trident distinguished itself as an airplane that represented the future of commercial aviation. Although larger stretched models were subsequently produced and were ultimately successful within the small market niche, the Trident was quickly relegated to the back pages of airliner prominence. As with many other British transports, the diminutive tri-jet from Hatfield was soon outdone by stronger competitors from the United States, which once again emerged victorious in world markets.

WELCOME ABOARD THE CONVAIR 990

By Mike Machat

The differences in this airplane become apparent even before you enter the cabin, for the door is shaped unlike any other in the world. Vertically straight on the left side, but tapered-in on the right, this windowless device is a marvel to behold.

Walking down the aisle to your seat, you notice the coach cabin's five-across seating configuration. As with the Convair 880, it's two on one side and three on the other—a configuration that won't be seen in other jetliners until the Douglas DC-9 enters service in 1965. Taking your seat just aft of the wing you look out the window and can't help but notice the 990's sleek and curvaceous "speed pods" mounted on the wing's inboard trailing edge. With the engines now started and whining in unison, the ground tug pushes your airplane back from the gate, and then the magic of this machine becomes readily apparent.

The somewhat firm ride while taxiing is more reminiscent of Convair's B-58 Hustler supersonic bomber. Like driving a Ferrari in second gear, you can't help but sense the potential performance of this airplane. Taking the runway, the captain pushes the thrust levers to their stops and nearly 65,000 pounds of thrust from four General Electric turbofans sends you bounding down the concrete in what feels more like a takeoff in a jet fighter. You notice the look of surprise on the faces of your fellow passengers as the 990 rotates smartly and climbs at a somewhat steeper angle than that "straight-pipe" 707 you flew on last time.

With flaps and slats retracted, the 990 now climbs swiftly to its cruising altitude. Soon the wind noise from the outside air rushing by your window at more than nine-tenths the speed of sound tells you that you're indeed flying aboard the fastest jetliner in the skies.

The 990 was the only commercial jetliner to utilize anti-shock bodies on the trailing edges of its ultra-thin wings. Added to take a continuous airflow over the upper wing surface, they lessened or delayed the shockwave that increased drag at speeds above Mach .80. The pods served as additional fuel tanks in all but the aft sections and also contained discharge nozzles for fuel jettisoning. (Jon Proctor Collection)

WHAT HAS HAPPENED SINCE

Air Canada Airbus A340. A Canadian airliner built by a European consortium serves long-range nonstop routes between North America and Asia, showing the ultimate globalization of the air age. (Mike Machat)

Our story ends in 1962 as intercontinental jetliners reach maturity, but commercial aviation continued to develop for many years thereafter. Smaller "regional" jetliners, larger "wide-body" jetliners, and even supersonic jetliners all took to the skies by the end of that decade. Perhaps the most graphic change in the industry is evident in the number of American airliner manufacturers. Of the five companies building commercial airliners in the United States at the beginning of our story, only one remains in business today.

Although our story ends with the introduction of larger and more refined fanjet-powered airliners, the continued evolution of air travel in the Jet Age bears mention as a fitting and proper ending to this book. By the end of the twentieth century, the airline industry had transformed itself from a "higher, faster, farther"

mentality to a "less is more" frame of mind. The proud post–World War II generation who led the endless quest for greater speed, range, power, and passenger capacity gave way to a more modern group of industrial thinkers who toiled to bring less operating cost, less fuel consumption, and less noise and pollution to the world at large. By the turn of the century, the torch of progress had been passed to a new digital generation of airliner builders and operators, although their numbers were definitely fewer than before.

Former titans of the airline industry who were pilots themselves or "airplane people" as well as businessmen, had also been replaced by a new breed of generic corporate leaders armed with MBAs and fiscal management skills that fit the newly homogenized corporate culture running rampant throughout the airline world and the world at large. Indeed, the only constant in this beloved industry became change itself. On the airframe and engine manufacturing side of the ledger, a myriad of companies worldwide began merging into seemingly unidentifiable corporate conglomerates. By the mid-1960s, proud names like Martin and Convair were gone, and other once-untouchable companies like Douglas and Lockheed were suddenly pushed to the edge of financial oblivion.

Pummeled by manufacturing problems and production delays exacerbated by jet-engine deliveries being diverted for the rapidly growing war in Vietnam, the Douglas Aircraft Company merged in a "shotgun wedding" with military manufacturer McDonnell in April 1967. Lockheed, whose turboprop Electra effectively bridged the gap from props to jets, was kept afloat until the advent of its L-1011 TriJet, bolstered through the lean years only by the company's successful military business. The biggest surprise, however, was that Boeing, once the undisputed underdog in the airliner manufacturing world, had now risen to the top of the pyramid by virtue of its undeniable success with the 707 series. This pioneering airplane sired an entire family of new jetliners, large and small, each one breaking barriers and establishing jet passenger service in new ways.

In October 1978, the Airline Deregulation Act was signed into law by then–U.S. President Jimmy Carter. This well-intentioned piece of legislation quickly turned the airline world on its proverbial ear. Although the noble intent was to lift restrictions on domestic routes and airfares, thus encouraging healthy competition, the result was rampant, unbridled route expansion, an explosion of new upstart carriers, and the end of many established airlines, all happening at unprecedented speed and on an unprecedented scale. The David-and-Goliath success story of tiny Southwest Airlines emerging as an industry giant was also written (although the carrier began operations in 1971), as it continued to thrive despite the challenges posed by Deregulation. However, there were many more tales of sordid failure as countless new upstarts tried to emulate Southwest's unique business model with little success.

America's domestic trunk airlines began to stumble while trying to compete on newly acquired overseas routes purchased from struggling Pan American World Airways—the same company once proudly called "The Chosen Instrument." By the end of the century, Pan Am, along with Braniff, Eastern, National, Western, and more than 100 regional and local airlines no longer existed, having been either merged into other carriers or plunged into bankruptcy and oblivion. TWA held on valiantly but then disappeared in 2001, with pieces of the company having been purchased by American Airlines. Today, only American, United, Continental, and Delta remain as the surviving U.S. "legacy carri-

ers," with Northwest—itself an amalgamation of older airline names—being merged into Delta as this book is being written.

In the late-1970s, a grim undercurrent also began to appear on the domestic airline scene with insidious acts of violence involving commercial aircraft. The casual inflight atmosphere of friendly visits to open cockpits and captains strolling down cabin aisles personally greeting passengers came to an end. Even airport access where a young wide-eyed kid could hang on a chain-link fence or stand on a sweeping observation deck was slowly replaced by a darker "future shock" world of beeping metal detectors, barbwire fences, and alarmed terminal doors. Back in the 1950s, a sinister wave of airliner hijackings and inflight bombings to collect passengers' life insurance swept the industry, but by the 1980s, a number of U.S. airline flight-crew members had been tragically shot inflight with the resultant loss of their airplanes and all the innocent passengers onboard.

Although violent hijackings and airliner losses from terrorist bombings had occurred overseas, the first subtle hint of international terrorism reaching U.S. shores appeared with a deadly bombing at New York's LaGuardia Airport Terminal at Christmastime 1975, when members of an Eastern-European political sect hid timed explosives in a public baggage locker. By the late-1990s, both Pan Am and Air India had lost Boeing 747s to explosive devices hidden in luggage containers with the loss of all onboard. Then, on a bright, clear September morning in 2001, the unthinkable happened as a stunned world witnessed on live television hijacked operational airliners being used as terrorist weapons for the first time in history. Three were flown into buildings and one crashed short of its intended target, but after the tragedy of September 11, the airline world—and the world in general—would never be the same again.

Smaller Jetliners in the mid-1960s

While the brilliant French Sud Caravelle became the Western world's first short- to medium-range jetliner in the late-1950s, a new flock of twinjet and tri-jet airplanes emerged in the following decade bringing significant advances in airframe, powerplant, and systems technology. In 1962 Britain's Hawker Siddeley Trident became the first new smaller jetliner to take flight after the original Caravelle, but it was another three-engine design from Seattle that truly launched medium-range jet-powered service two years later. Boeing's 727 was a revolutionary airplane when first flown, bringing jet speed, comfort, and convenience to smaller regional airports previously served by DC-6s, Constellations, and even Convair-Liners. With a total of more than 1,800 built in two basic models and operated by major carriers all over the world, the 727 was the most successful airliner ever flown at the time, becoming the undisputed DC-3 of the Jet Age.

After a failed marriage between Sud and Douglas to market the Caravelle in the United States, Douglas developed its own twinjet airliner called the DC-9, which entered service in 1965. Starting as a 100-seater known as DC-9-10, the basic design grew in typical Douglas fashion all the way to the Series 50. The next step was a rather big one, when the latest iteration became the DC-9 Super 80 with larger engines, wings, tail, landing gear, and a stretched fuselage that held up to 165 passengers. The most advanced airliner of its time, the Super 80 was renamed the MD-80 (MD standing for McDonnell Douglas, replacing the classic DC, or "Douglas Commercial" designation) and grew into the MD-90, and the shorter-fuselage MD-87. The final member of the family was originally called the MD-95, a name that morphed into the Boeing 717 when that company acquired McDonnell Douglas in 1997.

Meanwhile, in England, the newly established British Aircraft Corporation (BAC) designed a small twinjet for inter-European routes that eventually became a DC-9 competitor. Called the BAC 111, it entered service in 1965. Ironically, this airplane was flown in the United States, as well, by American, Braniff, and Mohawk to connect those carriers' smaller cities to their 707 and DC-8 trunk routes.

By 1968, Boeing was building a shorter, twin-engine feeder liner of its own called the 737, launched by Lufthansa and first operated in the United States by United Air Lines, ironically replacing aging Caravelles on United's routes. In a classic example of how dramat-

Bringing jet service to the world's smaller cities was the Boeing 727, which entered service in 1963. With more than 1,800 built, the 727 was to the Jet Age what the Douglas DC-3 was to the late-1930s—a machine that could make a profit for companies flying passengers to destinations all over the world. Many are still flying today. (Boeing/Jon Proctor Collection)

ically things can change in the airline industry, the modest and stubby little 737 grew in size, power, range, and passenger capacity over the years, and is now flying in its third design makeover, glass cockpit and all. With more than 6,000 delivered (and another 2,000 currently on order), the 737 has become the most successful single-aisle jetliner in history. To put all this in proper perspective, the latest version in the 737 series can carry more passengers over longer distances on two fewer engines and with two fewer flight crew than Boeing's original 707 could when first introduced in 1958!

Larger Jetliners in the late-1960s

Although public perception is that the Boeing 747 was the first airplane called a Jumbo Jet, that distinction technically goes to the McDonnell Douglas Super-60 family of advanced DC-8 jetliners. Douglas engineers at Long Beach created the world's first 250-passenger airliner by adding more than 37 feet to the original DC-8 fuselage, and then developing three versions of this new larger airplane by combining different engine, engine pylon, and wingtip designs to meet various airline requirements.

The first stretched model, the DC-8-61, simply added a longer fuselage to the existing DC-8-55 wing and engines. The DC-8-63 became the "Cadillac of DC-8s" by combining the -61 fuselage with a longer wing, new "flow-through" nacelles for its uprated fan-jet engines, and sleeker "cut-back" pylons for improved aerodynamics and drag reduction. By shortening the new longer fuselage and utilizing the Series 63 wing and engine configuration, the DC-8-62 was born, offering such ultra-long-range routes as New York to Hawaii nonstop for the very first time. Flown by United, Delta, Eastern, and National, plus Braniff, Air Canada, and a host of international carriers, the DC-8 Super-60 series brought a new paradigm of lower seat-mile economics to airline operators and passengers alike, setting the stage for the next big step in airliner development.

Responding to a U.S. Air Force request to develop a new giant jet airlifter, Boeing, Lockheed, and Douglas pushed the envelope of aircraft construction to new heights with the CX-HLS Program. General Electric and Pratt & Whitney did likewise for powerplant development. Standing for "Cargo Experimental, Heavy Logistics Support," this new mammoth aircraft was to be able to carry outsize loads on its main cargo deck, with accommodations for up to 90 passengers or relief crewmembers in compartments housed in an upper deck. A new generation of high-bypass turbofans would provide a then-staggering 25,000 pounds of thrust each to lift this beast into the air.

Although Lockheed won the CX-HLS contract with its C-5 Galaxy powered by General Electric

Ushering in the era of affordable air transportation for the masses, Boeing's 747 entered service in 1970. The dream of Pan American's Chairman, Juan Trippe, Pan Am and Boeing once again led the way to the next paradigm in commercial jet airliners, just as they did 12 years earlier with the Boeing 707. (Jon Proctor)

engines, all five companies involved managed to parlay their newly acquired design expertise into the creation of giant new engines and airframes suitable for commercial passenger use.

First off the mark was Boeing with its impressive new 747 designed to the specifications of launch customer Pan American. More than 230 feet long and with a wingspan of 196 feet, this four-engine Goliath carried up to 400 passengers in mixed-class configuration with an exclusive upper-deck lounge located above the forward fuselage, accessible via a regal-looking spiral staircase. Entering passenger service in 1970, the 747 went through the inevitable teething problems for integrating so large an airplane into the existing air-travel infrastructure. It emerged, however, as a highly successful airliner that provided affordable air travel to the masses and drove the basic cost of flying down to unheard-of levels. With more than 1,400 produced to date, the 747 soldiers on as the pioneering design that helped create the new age of affordable international air travel we somewhat take for granted today.

McDonnell Douglas entered the commercial jumbo-jet sweepstakes by complementing rather than competing with the 747. Responding to the needs of American and United for a widebody jet that could operate out of smaller airports like New York's LaGuardia, yet still carry 275 passengers on medium- to long-range stage lengths, McDonnell Douglas came up with a three-engine design called the DC-10. The new jetliner proved to be popular with the traveling public, but suffered a series of design-related accidents that tarnished the proud Douglas name. The DC-10 also became the Air Force's newest tanker named the KC-10 Extender, of which 60 were built, in addition to the 446 commercial DC-10s produced in Long Beach. Production ended with a follow-on design, a stretched, re-engined, glass-cockpit-equipped jetliner called the MD-11.

Last, but certainly not least in this trio of airliner titans was the Lockheed L-1011. The only jumbo jet to officially have a name, the L-1011 carried on Lockheed's stellar theme with the clever moniker TriStar. Considered a more advanced aircraft than the DC-10 from a systems standpoint, the TriStar was capable of Category III instrument landings and featured a center engine mounted in the aft fuselage fed by a streamlined S-duct air inlet. The L-1011 was ordered by TWA, Delta, Eastern, and Air Canada when McDonnell Douglas' senior management refused to negotiate the price of its DC-10 for these same airlines. In so doing, McDonnell opened the door to intense competition from its cross-town rival. However, only 250 L-1011s were built, and they were the last commercial aircraft produced by what is now the Lockheed Martin Company.

Supersonic Transports

As mentioned earlier, everyone in the airline industry fully expected to see the start of supersonic airliner service by the end of the 1960s. Both Boeing and Lockheed had impressive multi-hundred-passenger designs on the drawing boards; with the Boeing 2707 featuring a variable-geometry swing wing, and Lockheed's Model 2000 showing a raked double-delta planform. Both these mammoth machines echoed the lines of North American's radical six-engine XB-70 Valkyrie Mach 3 strategic bomber, which first flew in 1964. Unlike the Valkyrie, however, neither U.S. commercial Supersonic Transport (SST) ever made it past the mockup stage.

As public awareness of environmental problems associated with SSTs rapidly grew, the airplanes began to experience a reversal of fortunes. Provisional orders from the world's major airlines fell by the wayside as the rising drumbeat for ending America's SST development became too loud to ignore. In 1971, the Nixon Administration officially brought the U.S. Supersonic Transport program to a halt. Public concerns about the negative impact of such an aircraft, with its jarring sonic booms supposedly killing wildlife and high-altitude exhaust eroding the ozone layer, completely overshadowed whatever speed advantages any SST would be able to offer for a very small percentage of the traveling public. The factors of economics and passenger capacity won out over speed and technical supremacy once again.

That same year in Europe, however, a graceful and elegant-looking new airplane took to the air called simply, Concorde, the world's first and only successful supersonic airliner. Great Britain and France realized a decades-long dream to develop and fly such an aircraft, having studied the idea of a European-built SST as early

The world's only successful supersonic transport, the incomparable Concorde flew 100 passengers in the lap of luxury at altitudes of 60,000 feet and at cruise speeds of Mach 2.02—faster than NACA test pilot Scott Crossfield flew on his record run in the Douglas Skyrocket in November 1953. (Mike Machat)

as 1956, and pooling design resources in 1962 for a joint-development program known as the Super Caravelle. By 1967, British Aerospace Corporation and France's Aerospatiale had frozen a design that, although smaller in size than the American SSTs, promised supersonic travel for 100 passengers on overwater routes up to 3,000 miles, covering that distance at a cruising speed of Mach 2, or approximately 1,250 mph.

Not to be outdone, the Russians vowed to have the world's first SST in the air by the end of 1968, and achieved that goal with only hours to spare on the afternoon of December 31. The Tupolev Tu-144 also became the first commercial airliner to exceed Mach 2 in 1969, but without Concorde's advanced aerodynamic features the Soviet SST was never able to achieve the level of performance, comfort, and reliability required for the long-term passenger service enjoyed by its Anglo-French rival. Although built in several different and improved configurations, the Tu-144 surrendered the world's SST crown to Concorde after only a few short years in commercial operation.

Entering revenue passenger service in 1976, Concorde flew only with the national airlines of its manufacturing countries, British Airways and Air France. Although other short forays with interline agreements involving Singapore and Braniff International Airlines were briefly attempted, Concorde was ultimately relegated to flying from Europe to the U.S. East Coast over the North Atlantic, where effects of its sonic boom could be mitigated. After amassing a nearly perfect safety record over almost a quarter-century of flying, an Air France Concorde was lost on takeoff from Paris in July 2000. Despite fixes to the aircraft, severely reduced load factors and faltering post–9/11 world economics combined to bring Concorde service to an end in November 2003.

And Then There Was Only One

Boeing officially won the "survival of the fittest" game for airliner manufacturing in the United States by acquiring its weaker archrival, McDonnell Douglas, in 1997. Hence, the once-struggling, fourth-place builder of commercial aircraft from Seattle emerged as the lone survivor on the battlefield of broken airliner dreams, and today competes with only one other company in the world.

While Boeing recently ended production of its groundbreaking 1980s-era 757 and 767, the company still produces a robust series of airliners ranging from the "new-generation" 737 to the larger "next-generation" model of the venerable 747, called the 747-8. The 375-passenger Boeing 777, introduced in 1996 and still in full production today, was the world's first commercial airliner designed and manufactured totally with the use of advanced integrated computer systems, and is flown with an all-digital flight-control system. Extended-range versions of the 777 can fly literally between any two cities on the face of the earth.

After flirting briefly with the concept of a radical, canard-configured high-speed jetliner called the Sonic Cruiser, Boeing recalibrated its hopes for the future with the all-new 787 Dreamliner that is finally expected to fly in 2010. Rolled out of Boeing's Everett plant on July 8, 2007 (07-08-07), the aircraft suffered a nearly three-year delay in development, but this revolutionary all-composite airliner is expected to slash airline operating costs and overall fuel consumption by 20 percent over existing jets. With more than 800 orders on the books as this book is being written, the 787 is hoped to be an airliner for the ages.

The Emergence and Ascension of Airbus

Closely emulating Boeing's ascent to airliner legendry, a small consortium of European companies was established in 1970 with only a single aircraft design to its credit. Called the Airbus A300, this new jetliner emerged as a combined effort from existing aircraft factories in England, Germany, Spain, the Netherlands, and France, the latter country becoming headquarters for the new organization in the same facilities that produced the historic rear-engine Caravelle twinjet.

Building the twin-aisle, 250-passenger A300 was in reality a gutsy move made by a new aircraft manufacturer called Airbus Industrie. Although the concept of a widebody twin had been studied by McDonnell Douglas with a modified version of its proven DC-10, corporate management at McDonnell in St. Louis refused to allow its development, believing there would be little market demand for such an aircraft. A major stumbling block was that at the time, twin-engine commercial jets could not operate over large expanses of water. Airbus, however, saw the brilliance of the twinjet widebody strategy and rather adeptly stole the march on American manufacturers by perfectly filling the gap in available jetliner sizes. The A300 first flew in 1972 and entered service with Air France and Lufthansa in 1974.

With the advent of rules for extended overwater operations (ETOPS) in the early 1980s, twin-engine jets were allowed to fly overwater routes as long as they maintained a range within 20 minutes of landfall in the event of an emergency engine shutdown. The A300, along with Boeing's 767, soon found their calling. As engine reliability increased over millions of miles flown in service, ETOPS limitations were extended to 30, 45, 60, 90, 120, and eventually more than 200 minutes. Today, advanced 350-passenger twinjets, such as the Boeing 777 and Airbus A330, cover long-range overwater routes with ease, proving to be even more economical on certain stage lengths than earlier four-engine jumbo jets such as the Boeing 747 and Airbus A340.

Airbus Industrie gradually began to capture a growing share of the world's airline market, to the surprise of industry leaders worldwide. In addition to other advances, the European manufacturer demonstrated the world's first totally "fly-by-wire" airliner testbed at the 1986 Farnborough Airshow. Airbus stretched and shortened the A300B4 into the A300-600 and A310, respectively, and introduced its first single-aisle 150-passenger twinjet in 1987 with the advanced-technology A320, equipped with side-stick controllers and an all-glass cockpit. By stretching and shortening that aircraft, the company was able to develop an entirely new family of single-aisle jetliners, in much the way Douglas and Boeing did back in the 1950s and 1960s.

In 1991, the company expanded its widebody line with the addition of the A330/A340 duo—an innovative choice of either twin- or four-engine aircraft using the very same airframe! The four-engine A340 came first in 1991, setting long-distance records before it even entered service. The A330 twin soon followed, which was basically an A340 minus its two outboard engines. Fuselages for both models were then stretched into various versions best suited to customer needs carrying from 260 to 380 passengers.

By the early 1990s, the world's three remaining airliner manufacturers were all hinting at plans to develop the largest airliner ever flown. With world economic markets growing at a record pace, marketing mavens fully anticipated the need for vast fleets of 600-passenger Super Jumbos to begin plying air routes between Asia, Europe, and the United States. In a classic case of survival of the fittest, only Airbus emerged with a new aircraft, the 555-passenger A380 double-decker. This mammoth machine first flew in 2005 and, despite some early manufacturing problems, entered service with Singapore Airlines in 2007 and then Qantas and Emirates in 2008. Although anticipated markets never developed due in part to a sudden world economic downturn in early 2009, Airbus remains the sole builder of the only double-deck Super Jumbo airliner flying today.

Airbus Industrie officially overtook McDonnell Douglas as the world's number-two airliner manufacturer in 1983, but the airline world endured yet another shock when it was announced in 2005 that for the first time since the late-1950s, another aircraft manufacturer had outsold Boeing's commercial aircraft division. That manufacturer was none other than Airbus Industrie—known today as the Airbus Division of the European Aerospace and Defense Systems (EADS) Company. The colorful story of Boeing's rivalry with Airbus is certainly not over, and continues as we go to press.

Known as the first of the Super Jumbos, a factory-fresh Emirates Airbus A380 is seen on approach to LAX during a route-proving demonstration tour in August 2008. (Michael Carter)

SPECIAL SALUTE

to the
BOEING 707

The work of one of the true masters of modern American illustration, this epic Ren Wicks painting shows an imaginary inaugural gala for TWA's majestic new 707 complete with Hollywood premier searchlights.

TWA

N7317W

BOEING
707

In remembering the seemingly magical time when jet airliners first entered commercial service in October 1958, it is important to note that for the better part of the first year of operations, there was only one U.S.-built jet airliner flying, and only three U.S. flag or domestic carriers using it. That airplane was the Boeing 707. Hence, if you were standing on an observation deck at New York, Los Angeles, Paris, or London, this would be the only American jetliner you would ever see. Moreover, in certain U.S. cities celebrating the beginning of jet service at the time, there might be only one airline flying there in a 707.

For those of us standing by an airport chain-link fence in 1959, watching landing approaches on Aviation Boulevard at LAX in California or Rockaway Boulevard at New York's Idlewild, the scenario might be something like this: Seeing a four-engine propliner with red-white-and-blue propeller tips gleaming in the afternoon sunlight would signal the approach of a United Air Lines DC-7 Mainliner. Next would be a red-striped triple-tail Trans World Airlines Super-G Constellation, followed by a regional airline's twin-engine Convair Liner. All typical fare for dedicated airport brethren of the time.

Then, someone in the crowd would excitedly exclaim, "Look, there's a jet!" Wisps of smoke on the horizon would signal the approach of a jetliner that could only be a brand-new Boeing 707. Would the plane belong to Pan American, TWA, or American Airlines? As the aircraft came into view, the bright red-orange nose of the latter airline became visible, and soon, all 135,000 pounds of sleek bare-metal whistling tonnage would scream overhead with the wail of a thousand banshees. Unlike the national mood only a few years later, no one ever seemed to mind the noise. After all, it was a jet.

During a typical afternoon of airplane spotting, one might see only one or two 707s for every ten or twelve propliners, but the experience was well worth the wait. Another new sound often accompanied these swept-wing giants as they soared overhead only seconds from touchdown. It was an eerie sound with a ghost-like "wooosh" that would linger overhead after the plane flew by, and then, just as quickly as it appeared, would swiftly dissipate. On cloudy days you could actually see the cyclonic tube of air that created this sound. It was the turbulent vortices emanating from the jetliner's wingtips as they sliced through the air at then-unheard-of approach speeds of nearly 150 mph.

Welcome Aboard...

...this magnificent new Jet airplane. Yes, this is the newest, largest, and fastest Jetliner in the skies today. And its longer range assures non-stop flights over the Atlantic — in both directions. Even on the ground, every line of the **TWA** INTERCONTINENTAL **BOEING 707** — inspires confidence... and tells you here is the ultimate in travel speed and comfort. You notice at once the swept back wings... the absence of propellers on the four great pure jet engines and above all — the majestic size of this totally different plane!

Another facet of this new era in transportation was the marketing of these airplanes to the general public. Dramatic artwork and vivid color photography was incorporated into new brochures produced to create a sense of excitement and glamor for this dramatic new mode of air travel. Reflecting the 1950's genre of commercial illustration, images of cavernous passenger cabins occupied by handsome, well-dressed men and stylish women graced the pages of these brochures. Illustrations or photos of lavishly prepared foods being served to attractive passengers flying in the sumptuous cabin of a new jetliner conjured up images of elegant dining aloft while flying in the stratosphere at close to the speed of sound.

As mentioned earlier, one of the premier American illustrators of the day was Ren Wicks, founder of the world-renowned commercial art studio, Group West. As personal artist to TWA's Howard Hughes, Wicks was tasked with creating the trend-setting artwork that brought TWA's Boeing 707 to life years before the airplane entered passenger service. Wicks flew to all of TWA's major cities and photographed their respective skylines and cityscapes from helicopters to acquire the detailed reference material deemed so essential in achieving the realism seen in his artwork.

We, the authors, are honored to present these Ren Wicks images as contained in TWA's original 1959 Boeing 707 promotional brochure. They capture, in every sense of the word, the spirit of wonderment that pervaded the public consciousness about this burgeoning era of jet-powered commercial flight. From spacious cabin interiors to detailed flight galleys, to modern stylish lavatory décor—it's all here. Representing the Boeing 707 Intercontinental model is an original 1960 Lufthansa brochure for its Rolls-Royce Conway-powered 707-420, the first airliner in history to feature a wooden beer stein onboard for the First Class Senator Service.

Augmenting these beautiful brochures is a series of 16 photographs of 707s in various models and color schemes from, with few exceptions, the very first years of 707 service. You will note that this book is dedicated to the memory of Terry Waddington, a star member of the marketing and sales team for McDonnell Douglas in Long Beach, California. Terry was also a slide collector who amassed a sizeable archive of 35mm imagery from around the world that was second to none. By special arrangement, the Waddington estate has made these slides available to us, and we present them here in Terry's honor. We hope that through these historic original images, the Boeing 707 will once again come alive.

Appearing more like the passenger cabin aboard a much larger aircraft, this 707 forward lounge featured all the amenities of luxury and elegance aloft. Note the relative scale of the people compared to the airplane.

Just as a full-width mirror enhances the overall size of any room, this 707 lavatory looks absolutely spacious with ample shelf space and ultra-modern appointments and fixtures. A new jet airliner had to be impressive.

In a day and age when inflight service was the core of any airline's existence, a well-equipped and fully stocked galley was as essential to the overall passenger experience as a high-tech cockpit was to the pilots.

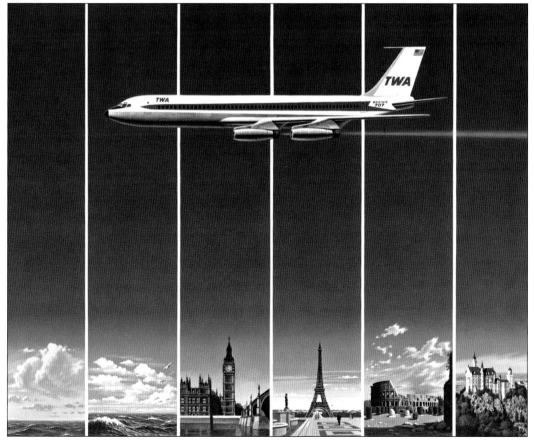

Following the rule that the peak use of illustration is to depict something unattainable in a photograph, artist Ren Wicks uses vertical stripes to symbolize the different time zones that are easily traversed by the 707.

Lufthansa's new Boeing 707-420 rolls out of the company's Renton facility on a typically rainy day in Seattle. This larger "Intercontinental" version of the 707 carried more passengers and flew farther than the 100-series.

Replacing the passenger's view of oil-splattered radial engine cowlings was this impressive vista of sleek turbojet engine nacelles connected by slim pylons to a swept wing. The wingtip probe was a radio antenna.

In today's world of $8 snack boxes, it may be difficult to fathom the thought of Lufthansa's Senator Service, and sumptuous meals being served at your seat. Inflight dining had all the amenities of five-star international cuisine.

Out of this galley—technically no less impressive than the pilot's instrument panels—come the fresh, crisp rolls, the grilled steaks, the ice-cold drinks and piping hot coffee to refresh you in midair.

Supplying delicious food and all the accoutrements was the responsibility of an Airline's Chief Chef. Although perhaps not onboard every flight, this enthusiastic cook looks every bit the part of TV chefs today.

Continental's "Golden Jet" service on the 707 literally set the standard for competition within the airline industry early in the Jet Age. Special custom-built motorized boarding ramps (lower right) were used to protect passengers from the elements before the advent of enclosed jetways. Shown here at Chicago's O'Hare, 707 Golden Jets brought jet transportation to other Midwestern cities not served by jetliners at the time. (Jon Proctor)

Pan American and Trans World Airlines were the largest Boeing 707 operators. Arriving at the International Arrivals Building (IAB) at New York's then-Idlewild Airport, Pan Am 707-321 carried the name Jet Clipper Splendid. Note the array of aircraft visible in the background, from an Air France 707-320 at the gate to a turboprop National Lockheed Electra, Pan Am DC-8, and even a classic American Douglas DC-6B taxiing in the distance. (Jon Proctor)

Braniff ad execs liked to refer to their "Big Jets," as reflected by the large red "-227" seen on this aircraft's aft fuse-lage. Combining the domestic body and more powerful engines from the 300-series, the -227 was unique to Braniff. The aircraft could fly faster than its 707-100 counterparts, and was able to carry heavier payloads out of "hot and high" airports such as Mexico City as well. This "Big Jet" is shown at Dallas' Love Field. (Robert Proctor)

Initially operating Rolls-Royce Conway-powered 707s, BOAC later acquired Pratt & Whitney turbofan models. Featuring the stylish new "speedbird" logo seen in metallic gold on the tail, the airline adopted a slightly modified livery from the midnight blue-and-ochre delivery color scheme seen on page 126. Note BOAC logos on the forward engine pylons, a carry-over from the airline's Comet 4 "slipper" fuel tank markings. (Jon Proctor Collection)

Air India also opted for Rolls-Royce Conway engines on its initial fleet of Boeing 707 Intercontinentals. Named Gauri Shankar, VT-DJJ is seen here in a handsome modified 707 color scheme being prepared for departure at Zurich, Switzerland. Although technically a turbojet, the Rolls-Royce Conway was known as a "bypass" engine, offering slightly higher thrust. It served as a precursor to the true turbofan engine. (Jon Proctor Collection)

Sabena Belgian World Airlines became an international 707 operator offering transatlantic service beginning in January 1960. This airplane's handsome color scheme, seen here at Orly Airport in Paris, was adapted directly from the design used on the airline's Douglas DC-7C intercontinental propliners before delivery of its 707s. The 707-320 carried 165 passengers and had a cruising speed of 600 mph. (Jon Proctor Collection)

El Al operated a weekly New York-Tel Aviv "nonstop" with its Rolls-Royce-powered Intercontinental 707s, but most trips stopped both ways at London's Heathrow Airport, where this picture was taken. Wearing a revised color scheme designed in 1971 for the airline's new Boeing 747 jumbo jet, this 707 serves as a nice example of how the airplane's classic lines look good even in more modern colors. (Jon Proctor Collection)

South African Airways (Suid-Afrikaanse Lugdiens), was known for luxurious in-flight services on its three 707-344s. ZS-CKC is seen here on push-back at London-Heathrow. Like other carriers, SAA later took advantage of Pratt & Whitney turbofan-powered Boeings, which were better suited to the airline's high-altitude destinations. The 707-300B series offered maximum gross takeoff weights of 330,000 pounds. (Jon Proctor Collection)

An original DC-8 operator, Eastern acquired 720s for short- to medium-range routes, chiefly on the U.S. East Coast and to Puerto Rico. Using both passenger boarding doors, N8712E awaits customers at West Palm Beach. The aircraft's attractive "arrowhead" motif was Eastern's ninth variation of its original jet color scheme designed for the DC-8 in 1960, and was applied to many of Eastern's older propliners as well. (Jon Proctor)

After leasing two 707s to enter the Jet Age, Western concentrated on turbo-fan-powered 720s, which were ideally suited for its route structure on the West Coast, across the Mountain region, and to Mexico. An updated "Indian Head" livery debuted on the type. N93152 is seen here being pushed back from the gate at Seattle-Tacoma International Airport. Note Beechcraft "commuter" at lower right. (Jon Proctor Collection)

In December 1961, Saudi Arabian flag carrier Saudia acquired two 720Bs originally built for Ethiopian Airlines, for use on flights between the Kingdom and destinations in Europe and North Africa. Showing the airline's dramatic change to jets, 720s replaced Convair 340 twins and DC-6As. The second 720 aircraft is seen here resting between flights at London-Heathrow, wearing its second distinctive dark green-and-gold livery. (Jon Proctor)

Beginning 707-328 service in January 1960, Air France added Pratt & Whitney turbofan models as it built up a large fleet of the Boeing jets. Chateau de Dampierre is shown here arriving at Boston's Logan International Airport, and was later retired and placed on permanent display at Le Bourget Airport in Paris. Fittingly, LeBourget was the destination of Pan American's inaugural 707 service in October 1958. (Jon Proctor Collection)

One of the first charter airlines to acquire newly manufactured jetliners, World Airways used convertible 707-373Cs worldwide, including civilian flights, military "MAC" charter, and cargo services. Shown in World's attractive red-and-white livery, a passenger flight arrives at Manchester, England. The 707-300-series' 143-foot wingspan can be seen here. Passenger capacity for MAC flights could reach 165. (Jon Proctor Collection)

Dwight D. Eisenhower was the first U.S. president to fly in a jet-powered aircraft, using a Boeing 707-120 operated by the Military Air Transport Service (MATS). This rare and historic photograph shows the turbofan-powered VC-137C (707-320B) Air Force One as it landed at San Diego on June 6, 1963. President John F. Kennedy was aboard the aircraft that day, barely five months before his tragic assassination. (Jon Proctor)

Colombia's national carrier Avianca received its first Boeing jet, a 720B, in November 1961, and acquired several new and second-hand examples before upgrading to intercontinental 707-359Bs, including HK-1402, seen here at the International Arrivals Building at New York's JFK in May 1968. It is interesting to note the use of mobile boarding stairs at a time when most Jet Age airports had more modern jetways. (Jon Proctor Collection)

Air Portugal was a relatively late customer for the 707, beginning service with the type in early 1966. CS-TBG, named Fernao de Magalhes, was one of the last commercial 707s to roll off the assembly line, and was delivered to TAP in March 1970. A total of 1,010 707s were built for the world's airlines and the military from 1958 to 1991. Military 707s flew for the U.S. Air Force, the Navy, NATO, and several foreign air arms. (Jon Proctor Collection)

RECOMMENDED READING LIST

Many excellent books and publications about all aspects of commercial aviation were consulted in the making of this book. In many cases written by the legends of our industry, these titles are available for more in-depth study of all the airplanes of the Jet Age.

Books

Andrews, C. F. and Morgan, E. B., *Vickers Aircraft Since 1908*, London, England, Putnam, 1969, 1988.

Arend, Geoffrey, *Great Airports, Kennedy International*, New York, New York, Air Cargo News, Inc., 1981.

Bedwell, Don, *Silver Bird, The American Airlines Story*, Sandpoint, Idaho, Airways International, 1998.

Bowers, Peter, M., *Boeing Aircraft Since 1916*, London, England, Putnam, 1966, 1968, 1989.

Davies, R. E. G., *Airliners of the United States Since 1914*, Washington D.C., Smithsonian, 1972.
—. *Continental Airlines, The First Fifty Years 1935-1984*, Woodlands, Texas, Pioneer Publications, Inc., 1984.
—. *De Havilland Comet, World's First Jet Airliner*, McLean, Virginia, Paladwr Press, 1999.
—. *Delta, An Airline and its Aircraft*, McLean, Virginia, Paladwr Press, 1990.
—. *Eastern, An Airline and its Aircraft*, McLean, Virginia, Paladwr Press, 2003.
—. *Lufthansa, An Airline and its Aircraft*, New York, New York, Orion Books, 1991.
—. *Pan Am, An Airline and its Aircraft*, New York, New York, Orion Books, 1987.
—. *TWA, An Airline and its Aircraft*, McLean, Virginia, Paladwr Press, 2000.

Francillon, Rene J., *Lockheed Aircraft Since 1913*, London, England, Putnam, 1982.
—. *McDonnell Douglas Aircraft Since 1920, Vols. 1 and 2*, London, England, Putnam 1979, 1988.

Gann, Harry, *Douglas DC-6 & DC-7*, North Branch, Minnesota, Specialty Press AirlinerTech Series, 1999.

Germain, Scott E., *Lockheed Constellation & Super Constellation*, North Branch, Minnesota, Specialty Press AirlinerTech Series, 1998.

Gradidge, J. M., *The Convairliners Story*, Turnbridge Wells, Kent, United Kingdom, Air-Britain Ltd., 1997.

Killion, Gary L., *The Martinliners – The Martin Twins, 202 to 404*, Sandpoint, Idaho, Airways International, 1998.

Luisada, Claude G., *Queen of the Skies – The Lockheed Constellation*, Raleigh, North Carolina, Ivy House Publishing Group, 2005.

Marson, Peter J., *The Lockheed Constellation*, Hazlemere, Bucks, United Kingdom, Air-Britain (Historians) Ltd., 2007.

Pearcy, Arthur, *Douglas Propliners – DC-1 – DC-7*, Shrewsbury, England, Airlife Publishing, Ltd., 1995.

Powers, David, *The Lockheed 188 Electra*, Miami, Florida, World Transport Press, 1999.

Proctor, Jon, *Convair 880 & 990, Great Airliners Series, Vol. 1*, Miami, Florida, World Transport Press, 1995.
—. *The Boeing 720*, Miami, Florida, World Transport Press, 1999.

Rummel, Robert W., *Howard Hughes and TWA*, Washington, D.C., Smithsonian Institution Press, 1991.

Scippa, Ray, *Point to Point – The Sixty Year History of Continental Airlines*, Houston, Texas, Pioneer Publications, Inc., 1994.

Stoff, Joshua, *Images of Aviation: LaGuardia Airport*, Charleston, South Carolina, Arcadia Publishing, 2008.
—. *Images of Aviation: John F. Kennedy International Airport*, Charleston, South Carolina, Arcadia Publishing, 2009.

Szurovy, Geza, *The American Airport*, St. Paul, Minnesota, MBI Publishing Company, 2003.

Stoller, Ezra, *The TWA Terminal*, New York, New York, Princeton Architectural Press, (undated).

Veronico, Nicholas A. & Larkins, William T., *Convair Twins – Piston Convair-Liners, Prop-Jet Turbo-Liners*, North Branch, Minnesota, Specialty Press AirlinerTech Series, 2005.

Waddington, Terry, *The Douglas DC-8, Great Airliners Series, Vol. 2*, Miami, Florida, World Transport Press, 1996.

Wegg, John, *Bluebirds*, Helsinki, Finland, Finnair Printing Department, 1985.

Periodicals

Architectural Record:
Hunt, Dudley, Jr., Idlewild Feature Issue, September 1961.

Airliners:
Mellberg, William F., "Friendships with a Difference," Nov/Dec 1997.
Proctor, Jon, "TWA's Connies," Summer 1989.
—. "Four-Engine Flagships," Winter 1991.

Airpower:
Machat, Mike, "Too Much Too Late," November 2002.
—. "Yesterday's Terminal of Tomorrow," November 2003.
—. "Battle of the Giants," August 2004.

Airways:
Davies, Ed, "Braniff's 'El Dorado Super Jet' 707s," October 2009.

American Aviation:
Parrish, Wayne E., "United's DC-7 Press Flight A Classic," May 1954.

Aviation Week:
Sweeney, Richard, "707 Imposes No Undue Stress on Pilot," October 13, 1958.
Garrison, Glenn, *Jets Spur Transatlantic Passenger Rise*, December 7, 1959.
—. "Jet Impact Felt in Transatlantic Market," November 7, 1960.

Flight:
June 1958 – Ninth Annual Local Air Service Issue.

FLYING:
January 1959 – Aircraft of the Jet and Turboprop Fleet Issue.

Journal, American Aviation Historical Society:
Betts, Ed, "Post-WWII Airliners," Summer 1997.

Newsweek:
(No author), "Now the Slick Medium-Range Entries Fly: Best, But Will it be Better," January 11, 1960.

TIME:
(No author): "Jets Across the U.S.," November 17, 1958.

WINGS:
Machat, Mike, "The Thoroughbred," February 2004.
—. "Tex Johnston, Boeing Test Pilot," April 2004.

INDEX

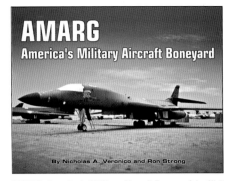
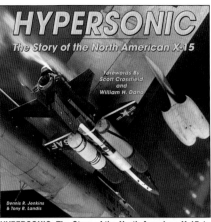
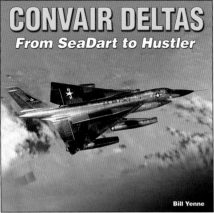
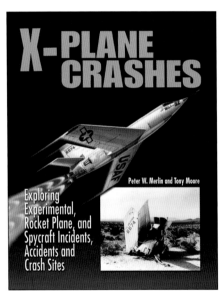

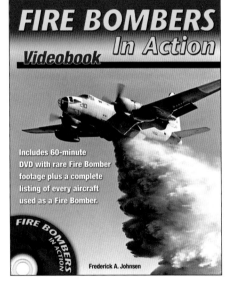